T0396654

HOW

TO

A STEP-BY-STEP GUIDE
TO SHARPENING YOUR SKILLS IN LOGO DESIGN

DESIGN

A

LOGO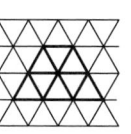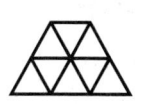

SendPoints

CONTENTS

004 | THE PROCESS OF
DESIGNING A LOGO

024 | BEYOND
THE LOGO

030 | THREE MAIN ELEMENTS
OF LOGO DESIGN

049 | 55 LOGOS
CASE STUDIES

235 | 99 LOGOS
AT A GLANCE

THE PROCESS OF DESIGNING A LOGO

1. INTERVIEW THE CLIENT

One of the major challenges in a project for the designer is to communicate with the client. In commercial design projects, the involvement of the client in the project is no less important than the expertise and the experience of the designer. Without proper communication with the client from the very beginning, the designer may often end up being trapped in a nightmare of endless revisions. A good design provides a solution to the client's problems rather than just providing a forum for designers to realize their own ideas and creative visions. Therefore, actively ensuring a full understanding of the client's purposes is a vital first step in delivering a good design outcome.

Before interviewing the client, designers need to do their homework, which means they need to have a good understanding of the client or the brand, including its history, products, target audience and the industry as a whole. With this essential background information, the designer can move on to preparing a question list for the meeting with the client.

It is important to give a good impression to the client in the first meeting. Therefore, the designer must stay confident and communicate with a clear logic, in order to convince the client that they are dealing with a trustworthy professional. The designer may be an expert in the world of design, but arrogance must never be shown, and the client's opinions must never be ignored. It is necessary to listen to the client, who, after all, knows more about the features of their products than the designer does. When the client fails to communicate his/her ideas accurately, the designer should listen carefully and offer guidance and suggestions as they take note of the information the client provides. After the meeting, the designer should go through these notes and carry out a careful analysis, so as to identify key words and concepts related to the design.

What is the client's current positioning?

What is the client's current positioning? What kind of corporate culture does the client currently have? What are the selling points of the products? What message should the logo communicate and what feeling is it trying to evoke in the customer? The answers to all these questions are invaluable for the designer as he/she seeks to get an understanding of the desired logo in his/her head.

What are the client's preferences?

Some clients may have their own ideas or preferences, so the designer should ask what kind of style, color, pattern etc the client prefers, or simply prepare some design ideas in different styles and let the clients pick what they like.

What are the client's needs?

Clients want new logo designs for different purposes. Some are trying to attract new customers, while others wish to update their corporate image and expand their market share. Some clients might have some specific requirements, like including the age of the company, or using some certain colors. The designer must take all such requirements into careful consideration.

What are the budgets, deadlines, and other requirements?

In order to ensure the project runs smoothly, things like budgets, deadlines etc must be discussed with the client at the very beginning, so as to avoid unnecessary disputes.

What media will the logo be used in?

If the logo is only to be used on web pages, the designer may have a preference for a certain color. However, if it is also to be used in commercial printing, the printing results and costs need to be taken into consideration when the designer is considering a design with complex effects.

2. DO THE RESEARCH

Not every client is fully aware of the trends in their industry and what their competitors are doing. The designer should note that the information offered by the client is typically far from exhaustive. In-depth online research will always be a necessary step to have a more complete understanding of the company.

1

Communication with staff is one smart way for the designer to gain some insight into the company. Also, the designer can carry out surveys with the target audience to learn more about their impressions of the company and its products, as well as their preferences in terms of color and style. Not all of the information will be reflected in the design, but it is all very helpful for the designer as they make decisions during the design process.

2

Feedback from industry professionals about the business, the products, the market prospects and the current trends in the industry can be very useful for the designer in terms of getting a good understanding of the positioning and specific features of the company.

3

The designer is expected to know about the client's competitors. It is important to have a thorough understanding of the similarities and differences between competing companies and their products. Detailed analysis of the competitors' logos — a breakdown of their advantages and disadvantages, their styles, etc. — can ensure that the final design has the necessary qualities to be successful.

4

The designer also needs to carry out research on existing designs. Reading books related to logo design and looking at design-related images and photos are a good start. When the designer can picture the logo in his/her mind, platforms such as Behance, Dribble and Pinterest may come in handy if he/she needs to search for similar or related works. This will also help with avoiding copyright disputes caused by the misuse of existing clip art or patterns.

3. BRAINSTORMING

After gathering sufficient information and carrying out extensive analysis, the designer is then ready to go wild with his/her imagination, and use brainstorming techniques in effective ways. If this is in a team setting, all members need to be encouraged to contribute.

Identify key words

The first step is to brainstorm around key words related to the logo — the more, the better. Then choose some of the more promising words for further exploration and discussion.

Embrace the ridiculous

During a brainstorming session, members of the design team may sometimes come up with some seemingly ridiculous ideas. Criticizing or dismissing such ideas can create a huge barrier that will block ideas and undercut morale. Designers should never underestimate the potential of any idea, as sometimes the most ridiculous ideas may turn out to lead down the most illuminating and inspired paths.

Make a mind map

The designer can make a mind map to try to connect the dots. With more details comes greater inspiration. As they write down key words to catch the spark of new ideas, the designer starts to focus on the next step.

Take notes

It is necessary to take note of all interesting ideas, no matter if they seem relevant or applicable or not at that moment because they may provide vital inspiration for the design at a future stage.

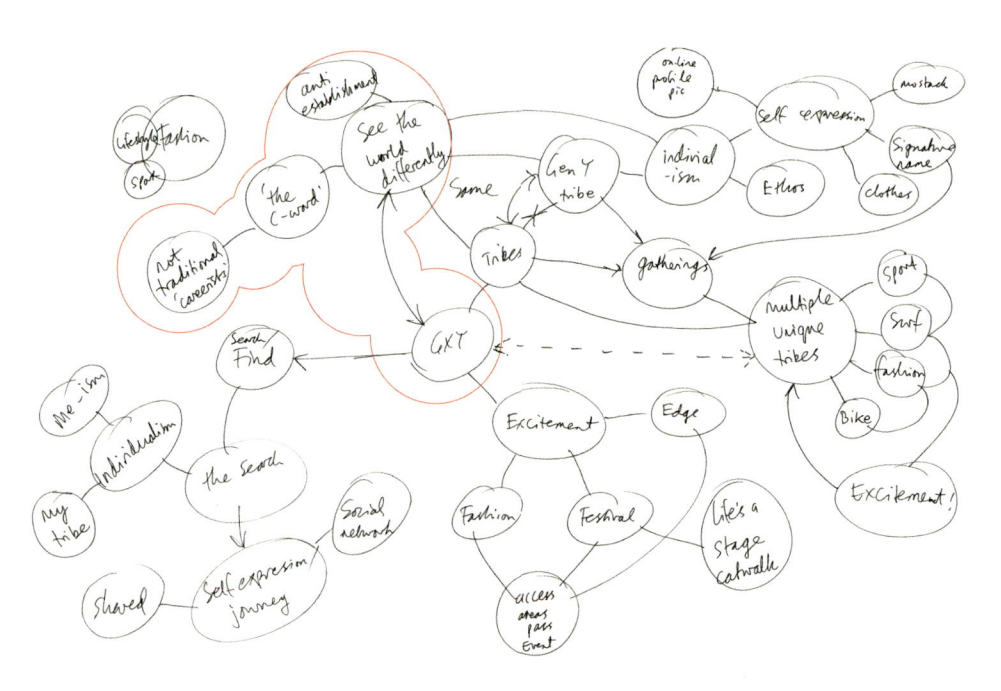

Design: Lachlan McDougall

4. SKETCHING

In order to catch the spark of inspiration, the designer should begin with sketching. This kind of sketching does not require any real accuracy or detail. The designer should sketch with a high degree of freedom, enabling him/her to record his/her ideas and inspirations. Sketches are flexible. Of course, the detail of sketches can be adjusted later to achieve a more satisfactory result. Throughout the entire design process, sketching is a great tool for designers in their ongoing efforts to make improvements to the logo.

Focus on One Thing

Typically, brainstorming will produce a number of key words, such as the name of the company, the features of the products, and perhaps, certain random elements from other sources, which may inspire the designer at the beginning of the project. For example, designer Tanja Deutschlaender was inspired by the word "Kiku" in the brand name she was designing for. The word sounded to her like a cock crowing, and so she ended up using a cock as the main body of the logo for the brand.

Design: Tanja Deutschlaender

Explore Different Ideas

The next step involves focusing on the initial inspiration, exploring different ideas and refining the initial sketches. The process of improving the logo design normally follows these three patterns:

1. Combining the initial inspiration with other key elements to make the logo more meaningful.

2. Changing the way the logo is drawn, arranged or shaped, which may lead in surprising directions.

3. Adding patterns or removing unnecessary decoration in the hope of achieving the overall desired effect of the logo.

This step often proves to be time-consuming, and sometimes needs the designer to produce more sketches, and to find the right detail to achieve improvement. So designers must be patient as they apply their expertise and follow their intuition to make the right choices.

Coop is a Danish supermarket chain, which aims to provide a convenient and friendly service to its customers. The designer manipulated the "C" from "Convenience" into a heart shape, so as to express the heartfelt feeling the company wished to convey to its customers.

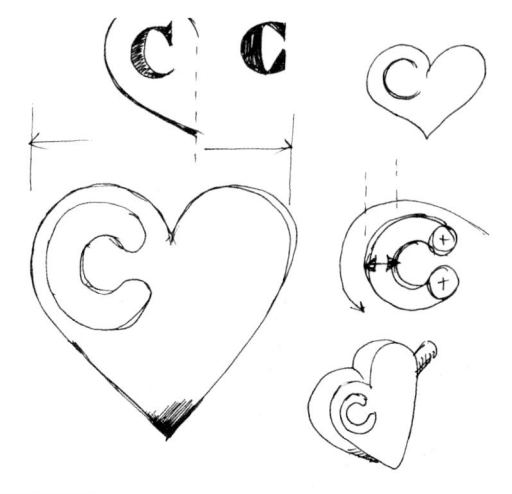

Design: Jess Andersen, Andreas Peitersen

Inspired by a traditional courtyard house on a rainy day, the designer has tried to sketch the scene from different angles, and eventually captures the moment when the raindrops fall from the eaves.

Design: Changhong Shi

Having made the decision to use a combination of three smiling faces as the main body, Andrea Vecera tried a number of different ways of drawing and arranging the faces in order to compare the different visual effects.

Design: Andrea Vecera

Different combinations may bring forth a brand new impression. In Chinese mythology, the dragon has nine sons, each of which has its own unique appearance. Drawing them on paper accentuates the brand's affinity with its customers.

Design: Weiping Li, Huapi Zheng

Dissatisfied with monotony of the pattern, Gabriele Malaspina uses a watery shading pattern to highlight the logo.

Design: Gabriele Malaspina

The clever use of the fork not only matches the "M" in the brand name, but also communicates indirectly the features of the restaurant.

Design: Pablo Chavida

5. DELIVER THE PRESENTATION

After finishing initial sketches, the designer needs to transform these sketches into a digital form, and present them to the client as a proposal. This is the best way to show and to try to sell the proposed design.

Refine the Sketch

The first step is to scan the sketches and upload them to the computer so that further detailed adjustments can be carried out. The designer can produce versions of the logo in different colors and with different angles to offer a range of options to meet the needs of the client.

Offer Potential Solutions

The designer should be clear about how they arrange their proposed solutions in the presentation. The most satisfactory solutions can be presented at the beginning, and similar solutions can be grouped together, which can allow the client to make relevant comparisons. Instead of piling on a large number of solutions, offering two to three is recommended.

Design: A-Side Studio

Design: Ilari Laitinen, Tuukka Koivisto

Normally, the proposal is presented in slides or dynamic diagrams.

Show how the idea evolves

Unlike other artistic works, logo design is simpler and more concise, so it's important for the designer to offer explanations to the client about where his/her inspirations came from and how his/her ideas evolved. Dynamic diagrams or flow diagrams illustrating how the logo developed enable the client to better understand the design.

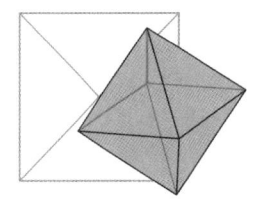

01 / Point Cut

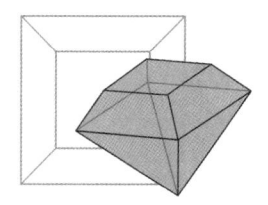

02 / Table Cut

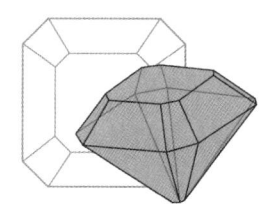

03 / Old Single Cut

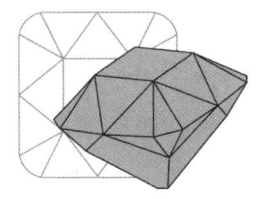

04 / Mazarin Cut

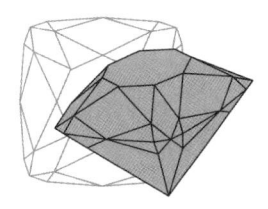

05 / Peruzzi Cut

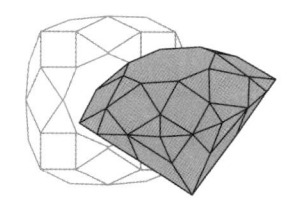

06 / Old European Cut

Design: Federico Landini

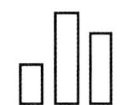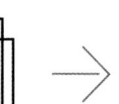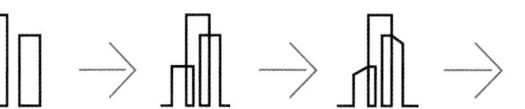

THE CALEB COMPANIES

Design: Peter Vasvari

Show the philosophy of the design

In addition to the quality of the design itself, the client will also be carefully focusing on whether the logo can reflect the company's values and culture. Showing and explaining the philosophy of the design can impress and convince the clients and win them over.

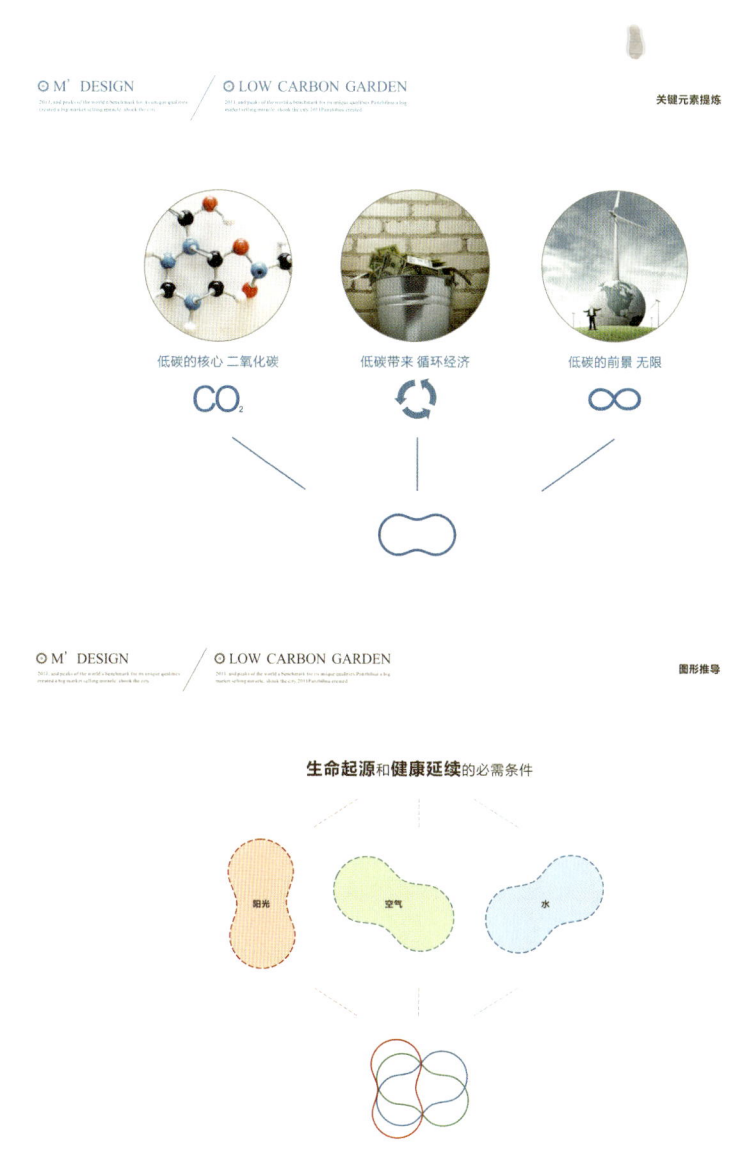

Design: Mengqiao Miao

Show the visual renderings of the logo

The designer can also include a number of visual renderings — for example iterations where the logo is applied to different materials and in different scenarios — to show the client how the logo would perform in the real world.

Design: Karl Randall

Prepare for the Presentation	After carefully preparing the slide, the designer should prepare for the presentation by organizing his/her language and thoughts to ensure they communicate his/her ideas fluently. This will also help the designer to become more confident.
Present the Design	The presentation is usually the second meeting with the client, and it is very important. The client is typically the owner of the brand and he/she can offer constructive feedback and suggestions from the perspective of the brand itself. Therefore, the designer has to make sure that the client understands fully the ideas behind the logo.
Receive Feedbacks	After the presentation, if the client is satisfied with the design, he/she might simply suggest some minor amendments, and the designer can move on to the next stage of making refinements to the design. However, if the client is not satisfied with the design, the designer must go over the requirements of the logo design again with the client, and figure out the reasons why the client is not satisfied, so as to avoid similar issues with future design proposals.

6. MAKE REFINEMENTS

The client, while accepting the initial proposal, may be dissatisfied with some details. Sometimes he/she may just accept the basic concept of the design, yet might still want to see some different versions. This step might often need to be repeated again and again, and this requires the designer to be patient as he/she listens to the client's ideas and gets an idea of what the client wants from the feedback.

Analyze feedback from the client

At the end of the day, the client is not a design specialist, so the designer must analyze the feedback from the client, and distinguish the good from the bad. For example, if the client insists that he/she wishes to use a certain pattern that is already in use in the industry, which may undermine its brand recognition, the designer should communicate this potential negative effect to the client. The client and the designer are on the same team. They both wish to maximize the benefit to the brand that the logo will bring.

Discuss with the client

If possible, it can be a very good idea to involve the client in the design. In this way, the designer can directly answer the client's questions and the client can gain a better understanding of the ideas of the designer and the development process of the logo. This involvement may help to increase the possibility of a satisfactory solution.

Go into detail

During this step, the refinement is mainly focused on details, like lines, fonts and colors. For example, the designer might add a curve, change the length-width ratio, or remove some elements from the logo design in order to better fit the brand image. When carrying out refinements like these, the designer should keep in mind the adaptability and the uniqueness of the logo.

Improve the solution

After the first presentation, the client may declare that he/she is satisfied with one of the solutions without providing any specific feedback. This situation requires the designer to look again at his/her design in order to find ways in which it can be improved. Very often, this will prove to be possible. It is never too late to have a good idea.

Finalize the design

The designer should again deliver a number of different solutions to the client in order to finalize the design.

04_1

04_2

04_3

05

06

Design: Alexey Zhurov

7. MAKE A STANDARDS MANUAL

All great designs are rigorous. Before finalizing the design, the designer needs to further standardize the drawing of the logo by using grids, auxiliary lines and precise circles. All kinds of problems may arise during printing and other applications of the logo if there are no standards in the size, scale, position, spacing and radian for the logo.

Set up Standards

Logo drawing can be standardized in the following three ways.

1. Use grids

Draw a grid with the same scale as the logo. The smaller the grid, the higher the accuracy, which allows for a clearer relationship among elements in the logo.

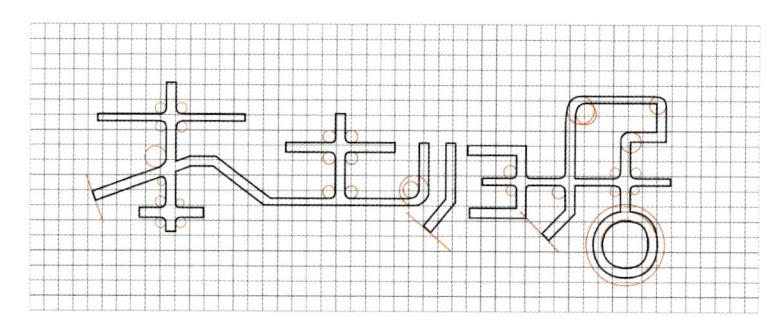

Design: Xitong Lu

2. Use scales

Set up a unit as a reference value to avoid distortion of the logo when it is scaled up or scaled down.

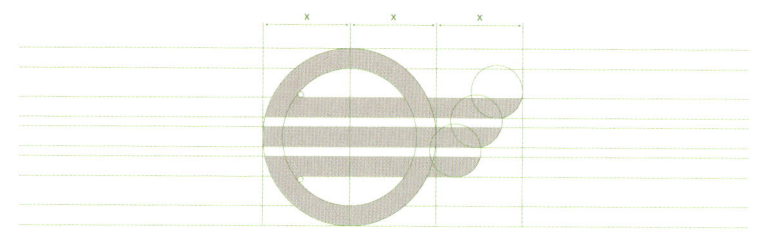

Design: BigO & Nugno

3. Use radians

Mark the correct angles and radians in the drawing. This method is especially applicable to logos with many arcs and oblique lines.

Design: Franck Juillot

Mark the Color Value and Offer Different Color Versions

Mark the RGB/Hex/CMYK color values or the Pantone Matching System numbers next to the logo to avoid color deviation during printing. This will also ensure that the selected color palette can be applied in different scenarios. In addition, the designer should provide different color palette versions of the logo — not just the original one. Grayscale, black-and-white and monochrome versions should also be offered.

File Formats

Apart from a vector file, the designer is expected to prepare the logo in other file formats, including a PDF file that is easy to transfer and save, an EPS file commonly used for printing, and a PNG or JPEG file used to view the image on a screen. Also, the designer should have backup copies of the file in case the original file is damaged or lost.

8. CREATE LOGO VARIATIONS

Good design should always offer excellent variations. Based on the original mark of the logo, the designer will sometimes need to create a range of variations with similar shapes and the same brand philosophy to accommodate different scenarios. This kind of variation ensures the flexibility of the logo, which is essential given that it will become perhaps the key standout feature of the brand.

Not all clients ask for logo variations, so, depending on budget and time constraints, the designer can communicate with the client as to how he/she would like to have any variations presented and how many variations are needed. Logo variations are an essential component of VI design (visual identity design).

Queen Rania Foundation

Queen Rania Foundation

Queen Rania Foundation

Queen Rania Foundation

Queen Rania Foundation

Queen Rania Foundation

Queen Rania Foundation

Queen Rania Foundation

Queen Rania Foundation

Design: Toormix

9. FINISH THE DESIGN

Presenting a satisfactory logo design proposal is not yet the final step. The designer should have the design printed to check the actual visual effect of the logo. It is very important that the printed outcome meets the expectations of the designer and the client.

After that, the designer needs to create a VI manual (visual identity manual) to ensure the consistency, and to show the client how to properly use the logo in all commercial the activities. A VI manual should include standards on typography, colors and the usage of the logo.

Design: Ed Price

BEYOND THE LOGO

The logo is a part of the VI system (visual identity system), which is a part of the corporate identity system.

Logo	VI System	Corporate Identity System

A corporate identity system normally includes the corporate logo, the desired typefaces and colors, alternative shapes and colors, recommended layouts, recommended combinations and incorrect usages.

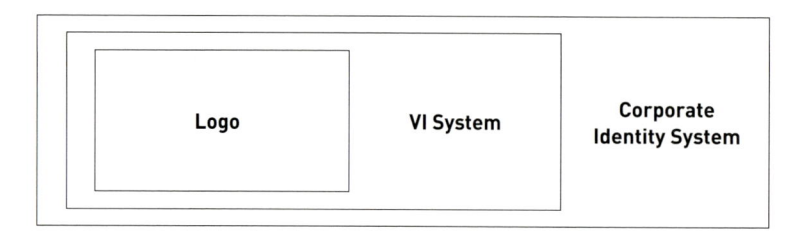

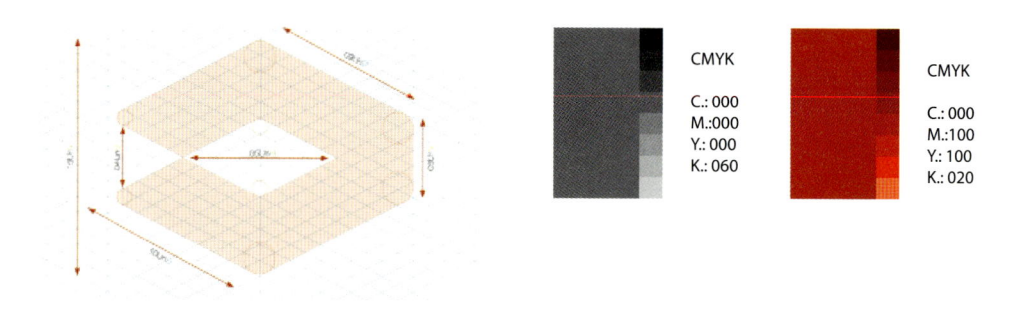

CMYK

C.: 000
M.:000
Y.: 000
K.: 060

CMYK

C.: 000
M.:100
Y.: 100
K.: 020

Design: Antonio Braz de Pina

THE CORPORATE LOGO

As logos are expected to represent the distinctive features of the company, their shapes and colors are supposed to be easy to recognize and remember. Elements in the logo can also be used in variations, so when designing shapes, and selecting colors and fonts for the logo, the designer can think about how these elements can help to create the variations.

Design: tegusu

DESIRED TYPEFACES

The designer should select a typeface that complements the logo, or create one using elements from the logo. A desired typeface normally refers to the text type, which, for example in China, includes both a Chinese and an English typeface, or sometimes it just refers to a decorative typeface.

Design: Johan Debit (Brand Brothers)

DESIRED COLORS

The desired color can be the corporate color, as it normally comes from the company's logo. So when applied in materials, it goes perfectly with the logo, creating a strong visual harmony. When the desired color is decided, the tone of the color scheme for the whole visual identity is basically set.

Design: Jeroen Van Eerden

ALTERNATIVE SHAPES AND COLORS

Alternative shapes can be derived from the logo through simplification or distortion, allowing the logo to be adapted to different scenarios. Alternative colors can be selected according to a given color palette to enrich the design when it is felt to be not sufficiently colorful.

Design: Johan Debit, Jean-Remi Massery

RECOMMENDED LAYOUTS

A recommended layout is needed if the client wishes to apply the corporate logo to various items ranging from office supplies, web pages to apps. A consistent layout scheme reflects the professionalism and stability of the brand and gives a good impression to customers.

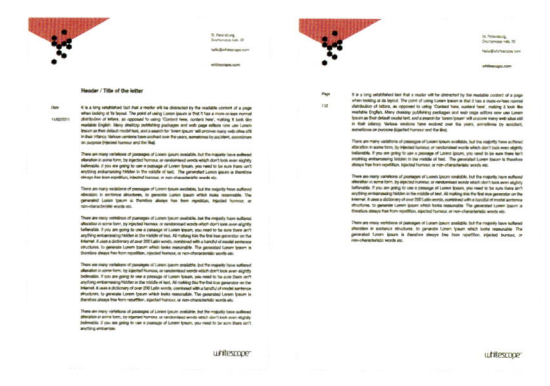

Design: Federico Landini

RECOMMENDED COMBINATIONS

A logo is expected to accommodate different scenarios, so it is necessary for the designer to offer various recommended combinations of marks, types, and alternative shapes.

Design: Zibin Florian Loi, Thilo Schinkel

INCORRECT USAGES

Apart from recommended combinations, the designer should also list incorrect usages and give examples. Incorrect usages of the logo, if any, should be prevented from ever taking place.

Incorrect usages of the logo include:

1. Using recommended combinations without the selected typefaces
2. Using recommended combinations in colors other than those selected
3. Combinations are not in desired arrangements
4. Use of logo with unauthorized background colors

Design: Jon Ander Pazos

THREE MAIN ELEMENTS OF LOGO DESIGN

The core of a visual identity is the VI system, while the core of VI design is the logo design. It can be said that the logo is the visual element that first establishes a bond between a brand and its audience. So where should the designer start in designing the logo? A good start would be to focus on the three main elements: typography, shape and color. There are three main kinds of logo — the one focused on shapes, the one focused on words and the one focused on both shapes and words. Slight differences in any of the elements produce different visual effects, so typeface, shape and color are all very important for a logo. Although a good logo may not necessarily include all three elements, clever and appropriate use of these elements in a way that suits the design can help to achieve an optimal effect in visual communication and can make a lasting impression on the audience.

TYPOGRAPHY

Words, as communicative symbols established by use and convention, are among the most direct expressions of human thought. Changes in the form of the words can fundamentally affect the way in which the words communicate. The proper use of typefaces can enable a brand to communicate in a meaningful way in terms of its visual results. If a designer develops a unique typographical design, it can not only give a logo an aesthetic power, but also help to visually manifest the brand's attributes, product features or philosophy.

TYPOGRAPHY CLASSIFICATION

Logo designs involve a variety of typefaces, among which serif and sans serif are the most commonly used.

Serif

A serif font is a font with small lines, strokes or extensions at the end of its longer strokes. Serif typefaces are usually used for body text because they are elegant and very easy to read. Designers tend to use them for brands with long and rich histories or to highlight artistic beauty. In Chinese, serifs are normally called Songti. Their delicate and neat structure makes them ideal for use in design.

Design: Eggplant Factory

Design: Diana Coe

Sans Serif

A sans serif font is a font that does not have serifs, small lines, strokes or extensions at the ends of its longer strokes. In Chinese, sans serif fonts with sharp angles at the corners are called Heiti, and those with soft curves at the corners are called Yuanti. This kind of highly recognizable typeface impresses the audience with its conciseness and formality and is suitable for brands either seeking to project a metropolitan style or to highlight their technological elements. Heiti is rather eye-catching and elaborate, while Yuanti is softer.

Design: thonik

Design: the brandbean

LETTER SPACING

Letter spacing refers to the horizontal spacing between text characters. Different letter spacing will cause differences in the density of the line and the text. Adjusting the letter-spacing value can either cause characters to spread farther apart or bring characters closer together, and thus, it affects the logo style. Tight letter spacing makes the text seem more formal, but if the spacing is too tight, the letters will overlap to the point where the word(s) may be unrecognizable. Wide letter spacing causes the text to appear more edgy and dynamic, but when it is too wide, the letters will be so far apart that the word(s) will appear like a series of individual, unconnected letters. The designer should take the brand features into consideration, and use letter spacing carefully.

Design: Federico Landini

Design: KOM Design Labo

FONT WEIGHT

Font weight choices are an important way to communicate the brand philosophy. The use of a bold font weight creates a sense of strength and security, highlighting the trustworthiness of the brand. On the other hand, a light font weight gives an impression of gentleness and softness, and it is the choice of many young brands. The font weight also needs to be consistent with the logo style.

Design: Vinković, Goran Šoša

Design: Supercake (Srl)

LOGOS FOCUSING ON TYPOGRAPHY

***Wordmark/
Logotype***

A wordmark or logotype is a font-based logo that focuses on the name of the business or the brand alone, communicating the brand's information in a rather direct way. Wordmarks are applicable to brands with a specific name of moderate length.

Design: Hermes Mazali

| **Lettermark** | A lettermark is a logo that consists of letters, usually brand initials or first letter. Many large organizations and multinational companies choose to use this type of logo. For example, the logo of the electrical services provider, New Gisborne Electrical, reminds people of its name and the services it provides, and it is also easy to remember. |

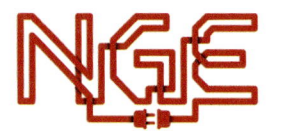 **NEW GISBORNE ELECTRICAL**
Servicing Macedon Ranges + Western Suburbs

Design: Nathan Barrow

| **Keyword Logos** | A keyword logo normally focuses on a keyword of the brand name, or some key word or key phrase from the brand philosophy. For example, a Croatian resort hotel chose the keyword "More" to highlight its brand philosophy — in the sense of "we have much more to offer than you expect", in the hope of attracting visitors. |

Design: Boris Ljubicic

KEY POINTS TO REMEMBER FOR TYPOGRAPHY IN LOGO DESIGN

Whether using an existing font or creating a brand new one to help the brand to stand
out, the designer should pay attention to the following key points.

***Go with the
Style of the
Brand***

Only by having a comprehensive understanding of the brand and its features can
the designer create a logo that matches the brand philosophy, so as to maximize
the value of the brand. Café Con Leche as a brand values leisure, and so, the type
in its logo is expected to be relaxing and delightful. In the logo design of the Jewish
Museum, the designer adopts a geometric grid that follows the pattern of the Jewish
symbol, the hexagram, to create a dynamic wordmark that shows its ambition to keep
up with the times.

Design: Emicel Mata

Design: Sagmeister & Walsh

***Be Highly
Recognizable***

It is important that fonts in logos look good and special, but legibility also counts . One
of the basic functions of words is to communicate information, so fonts that cause
difficulties in reading can never be anything but a failure. A good logo design, apart
from requiring a level of ingenuity, must feature a clear font structure.

Design: Roger Lara, Lucía Nolasco

Design: Pablo Chavida

Meet the Aesthetic Needs

Usually, a specially-designed typeface is often appealing and eye-catching and it can meet the aesthetic needs of the public. For example, Mind Design, inspired by locks of hair, by magazines from the 1980s and by rolled-up books, created this unique and vibrant wordmark design for Znips, a London-based hair salon.

Design: Mind Design

SHAPES

Shapes are a universal visual language created by people on the basis of common life experience. Even without words, the audience can understand the intended meaning communicated by the shape in the logo. If he/she wishes to use a shape design in the logo, the designer must have a strong understanding of the features of the brand from which he/she can figure out an appropriate way to fully interpret the brand philosophy using a shape.

SHAPES IN LOGOS

Representa-tional Shapes

Representational shapes refer to shapes that are not abstract, and are highly recognizable to the audience. In logo design, a restaurant that uses a fork shape, or a publishing house that employs a book shape are both examples of brands showing their business sector through the use of representational figures. Shapes of animals and plants help to establish an environmentally friendly and balanced image, and deliver a feeling of culture and refreshment. Benua Farm, a family restaurant located on a dairy farm, uses a figure of a cow in its logo to represent the origin of the brand. Cilsoie, a handcrafted jewelry brand, uses a figure containing foliage and a handcrafted ring in its logo to show the ingenuity of its craftsmanship and the brand's passion for life.

Design: Denk Studio

Design: Anoniwa

Abstract Shapes	Abstract shapes used in logos tend to impress and inspire the audience with the simplicity and uniqueness of the brand. Abstract shapes in logos can be geometric figures or irregular shapes. Moving, scaling and rotating two-dimensional shapes would not change their properties. A rectangle, with its lines and right angles, makes people feel secure and gives a sense of reliability; triangles stand for balance and stability; circles and ovals that can be finished in one stroke usually give people a feeling of eternity and mystery. Nordic Food, a food company from Denmark, uses four different lines in its logo to indicate the four elements — earth, fire, water and air, implying that though the four seasons come and go, a combination of different elements can make a satisfying whole. Both of these meanings are represented by the circle in the logo.

NORDIC FOOD

Design: de+st studio

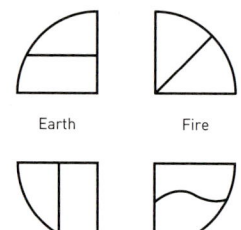

Earth   Fire

Air   Water

HOW SHAPES IN LOGOS WORK

By Repre- senting Something	Designers can use shapes that directly relate to the brand. For example, pet hospitals might use cat and dog shapes or ice cream shops might employ an ice cream shape in their logos to represent their business field.

Design: Peter Vasvari

Design: David Lawlor

By Implying Something

Designers can use shapes related to the brand to imply its philosophy. Adamo Music, a music management company, uses a heart shape and a sound wave to imply its love for music. The logo of Teatro & Punto consists of simple geometric shapes which resemble the tip of an ink pen and the stage, hinting at its main two domains: literature and theatre.

Design: Martine Lindstrøm

Design: Javier Muñoz Poblete

By Highlighting Something

The designer can impress the audience with a strong visual impact to highlight the philosophy of the brand by using concise abstract shapes and simple words. The logo of the Imperial War Museums features a rectangle cut into three trapezoids. Such a distortion highlights the huge impact of war on people's lives.

Design: Hat-trick Design

KEY POINTS WHEN USING SHAPES IN LOGO DESIGN

Closely Relate the Logo to the Brand

Shapes in logos should be closely related to the name, product or service of the brand, so as to maximize the benefits of marketing and promotion. Party and activity planning company, Diamond at Diamond Management makes use of the shapes of diamonds and vines in its logo. The elements are not only closely related to the business of the company, but also graceful and elegant. Kawa, a coffee shop app, follows a similar pattern by combining a coffee cup and a Wi-Fi icon — elements closely related to its business — with its brand name also incorporated into the logo.

Design: Gatis Cirulis

Design: tegusu

www.getkawa.com

Ensure the Logo can be Applied to Targeted Materials

When making use of shapes in a logo design, apart from the brand characteristics, the designer should also take into account the size and features of the materials that the logo might be applied to, so as to avoid any distortion of the logo. The city logo of Kyiv, the capital of Ukraine, is an example of a logo that can be perfectly applied to a whole range of contexts and materials, like ceramics, textiles and paper.

Design: Viktor Konovalov, Nataliya Strelchenko, Yuriy Husinskiy

COLORS

Color directly or indirectly influnces consumer behavior and impressions. Research by Colorcom shows that it takes only 90 seconds for consumers to generally evaluate a product, and 62%~90% of their evaluation is based on the colors of the product. Therefore, when designing a logo, the designer should take great care to choose a color palette that really complements the features of the brand in order to attract the audience and to better promote the brand.

THE THREE ELEMENTS OF COLORS AND COLOR TONE

The three elements of color are hue, saturation and brightness. They are indivisible, which requires the designer to pay equal attention to each of them when thinking about the use of color in the design.

Hue   Hues denote qualities that can be differentiated by color words such as red, orange, yellow, green, blue or purple.

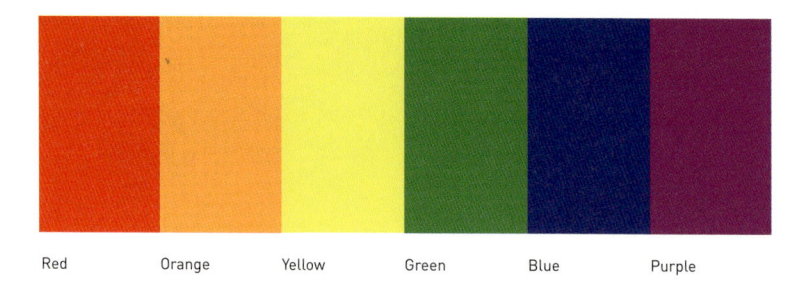

Red   Orange   Yellow   Green   Blue   Purple

Saturation

Saturation refers to how vivid, rich, or intense a color is. It is controlled by the amount of white added. As the saturation increases, the colors appear more pure. As the saturation decreases, the colors appear more washed-out or pale. Saturation is not applicable in black and white. Differences in saturation can lead to different visual results. The logo of Shenzhen Universiade, with its saturated color combination, stands out and gives people a lively impression. The color palette of Wrapaper's logo is desaturated, and in the end, it communicates a rather refreshing feeling.

Design: Jiasheng Chen

Design: Peter Vasvari

Brightness	Brightness, also known as lightness, is the relative lightness or darkness of a particular color, from black (no brightness) to white (full brightness). Thus, adding white will make a color brighter, while adding black will make a color darker. Changes in brightness will deliver a range of varied colors. For example, Fernanda Barbato designed this logo by controlling the brightness of the color in the iceberg shape.

Design: Fernanda Barbato

Tone	Tone generates an intuitive color impression or image resulting from a complex overlaying of brightness and saturation. Tone is described in terms of attribute pairs such as light-deep, bright-dark or strong-weak according to the values of brightness and saturation. Color palettes in the same tone, in similar tones or in complementary tones will lead to widely different results.

Design: Hermes Mazali

THREE MAIN ELEMENTS OF LOGO DESIGN

COLOR SCHEMES

Color combinations and schemes are quite diversified in design. Yet in order to come up with an appropriate color palette, a comprehensive understanding of the relationships between colors is required. The color wheel provides a visual representation of colors arranged according to their chromatic relationship.

12-Color Wheel

Monochrome   A monochrome logo design is based on a single hue. For logos that use complex forms like portraits, using monochrome can give the logo a concise, deluxe appearance. Also monochrome font-based logos can be more eye-catching.

Design: Masaomi Fujita

Design: Roger Lara, Lucía Nolasco

Analogous Colors

Analogous colors are colors that are next to each other, forming an angle that is less than 90 degree in the color wheel. Analogous color schemes often have a dynamic and harmonious feel.

Design: Jacek Janiczak

Design: Diana Egri

Complementary Colors

Complementary colors are opposite colors forming an angle of 180 degree in the color wheel. A split complementary color scheme combines a primary color selected from the color wheel with two analogous colors as its complement. The sharp contrast presented by complementary colors can strongly stimulate viewers' senses. Such a color scheme is quite modern and fashionable, and is particularly applicable to emerging industries and the Internet service sector.

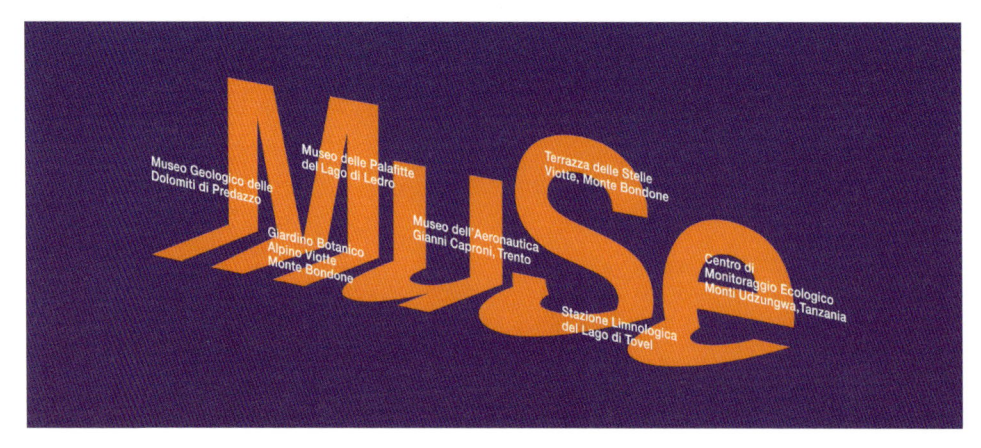

Design: Harry Pearce

| **Contrasting Colors** | Color schemes of contrasting colors are varied. Contrasting colors can be any color combination from an angle of less than 120-200 degree in the color wheel. Changes in the size of the colored area or brightness would create different visual effects. Logos in contrasting color schemes tend to be vibrant and impressive with a clear focus. |

Design: Oksal Yesilok

KEY POINTS IN USING COLOR SCHEMES IN LOGO DESIGN

| **Combine Colors with the Brand's Features** | Each color gives people a certain impression and feeling, which can affect consumer behavior. The designer should take into account the features of the brand and its target audience so as to deliver an appropriate color scheme for the logo that will build up the brand image. Cleaning company Hanamizuki uses blue, a color that stands for cleanliness and purity in its logo. The City College of New York uses purple which symbolizes a sense of reverence, and depicts of something sacred to communicate the essence of academic life. |

Design: Qiyao Tang, Junyao Huang, Xiangjia Wu, Yi Wang

Design: Menos es Más

Consider the Visual Result of the Color Scheme

Once the colors that match the brand's philosophy have been chosen, the designer needs to consider the visual result of the chosen color scheme. For example, logos in light colors or gradient colors require the designer to pay extra attention to how the logo will appear on printed materials.

Design: Karen Cantú

5 LOGOS

CASE STUDIES

Studio: Made&Co. / Designer: Cing Yu Chang

CARPE DIEM CO.

Carpe Diem Co. is a women's clothing boutique in Taiwan, China. The designer created a calligraphic logotype, which is free and elegant in appearance, in order to adapt to ever-changing fashion trends and also to represent its promise of high quality. The logo mark manages to reflect the brand's efforts to integrate a stylish classical spirit with everyday outfits by combining the initials and putting them in an oval frame — "Honestly, Truly, Completely".

1

2

Carpe diem

Carpe diem

Carpe diem

3

PANTONE 7546C
C12 M10 Y14 K0
R215 G212 B194
#D7D4C2

Carpe diem

PANTONE 172C
C0 M80 Y90 K0
R222 G84 B40
#DE5428

HONESTLY TRULY
DC
COMPLETELY

PANTONE 7546C
C88 M57 Y27 K65
R37 G55 B70
#253746

HONESTLY TRULY
DC
COMPLETELY

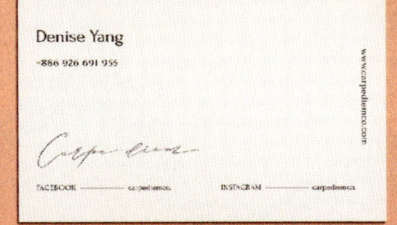

Honestly
Truely
Completely

Cloth aren't going to change the world.
The women who wear them will.

Designer: Hermes Mazali

BEDUKA

Beduka is an online platform that helps young students to find their ideal future career. The main body of the logo is the initial of the brand name "Beduka", with the "B" shaped into an open book icon, representing learning.

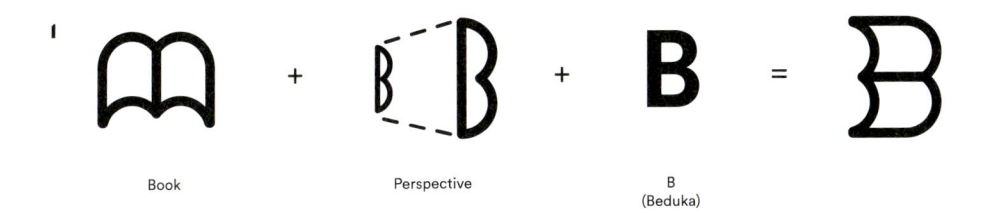

Book

Perspective

B
(Beduka)

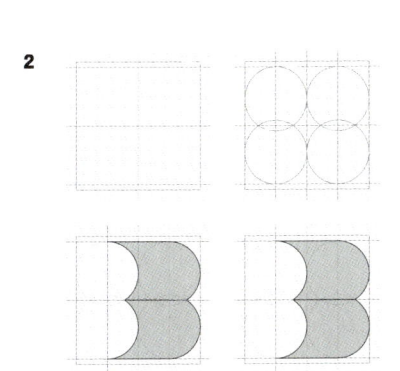

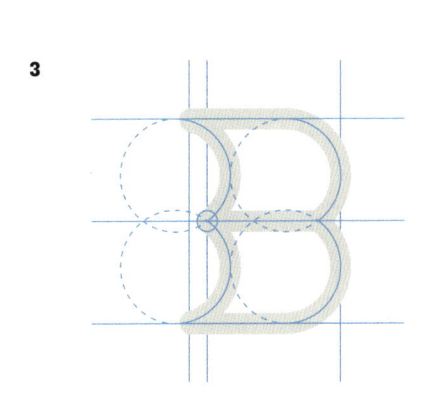

The designers created a compact yet smooth handwriting font, the structure of which is based on circles. The red color communicates the energy and passion of Heros, while the black represents steadiness. Together they form a modern and balanced brand image.

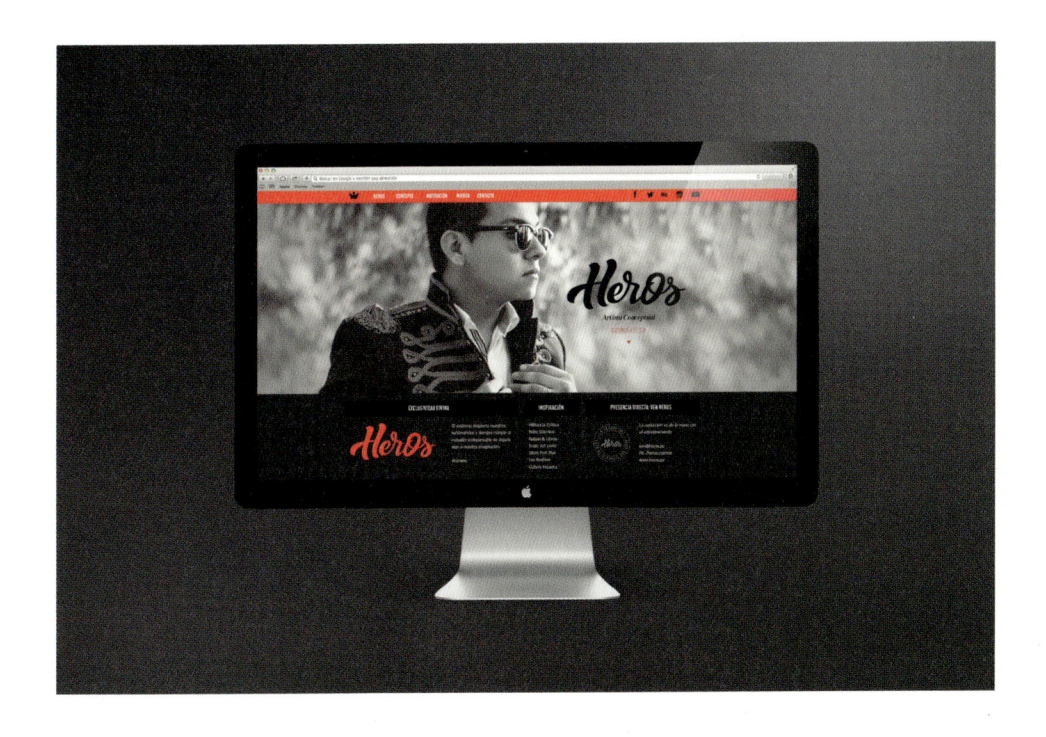

La sexualidad está
al servicio del Arte.

HEROS
ARTISTA CONCEPTUAL
DE LA ERÓTICA

hola@sirheros.com
FB: sirheros

www.sirheros.com

(f) (y) (@)

HEROS

ARTISTA CONCEPTUAL
DE LA ERÓTICA

*La sexualidad está
al servicio del arte.*

hola@sirheros.com
FB. sirheros

www.sirheros.com

Signo de Levine
COSMOERÓTICA

Mira, no ves que se entris,
la noche está tibia y yo a tus pies.

Mientras tú sientes que vuelas,
yo sigo en la espera de tu sutil calidez.

Porqué tue cambiamos los dos,
te pierdo y no encuentro razón.

Dima, que no es infalible, que nuestra ruptura
tiene solución.

Regálame tu sensual olvido,
para seguir cautivo de este deseoso burdel.

Hoy estoy pensando en ti.
Hoy te estoy haciendo feliz.

Mientras, yo siento que llegas
y me abrazas y te vas,
sin decirme por qué.

Yo solo quiero tenerte
en mi pecho otra vez,
para poder decirte,
que esto no puede ser.

Oh que esto no puede ser.

- Solo -

Cierra la puerta y vante,
cierra los ojos y bésame,
que quiero sentirte
en mis brazos otra vez.

En mis brazos otra vez.

Sienta, tu ausencia se siente,
cuando te escribo esta canción.

*La sexualidad está
al servicio del Arte.*

HEROS
ARTISTA CONCEPTUAL
DE LA ERÓTICA

(f) (y) (o)

FIGO

As a furniture design brand, Figo highlights simplicity and efficiency. Based on these values, the branding mainly aims to strike a balance between elegance and playfulness. Inspired by the bent steel plate, the main material used in the company's products, the designers integrated the shape into the logo design. The logo presents a smart yet relaxed brand image, and the dot added to the top of the letter "I" provides the key element that creates the lively dynamism of the logo.

1

FiGO. FiGO.

2

SALÓN SOCIEDAD

Salón Sociedad is a renovated hall located inside the Sociedad Cuauhtémoc y Famosa (SCYF) complex, a club for Heineken Mexico's staff and associates. The visual system, covering a series of illustrations, icons, and old photos of the complex, is based on elements inspired by the heritage and nature of the complex. The inspiration for the typographic logos comes from typefaces and layouts from the time of the establishment of the SCYF, and the icon of the arch represents the renovated hall. Such a variable logo system reflects a free and flexible environment.

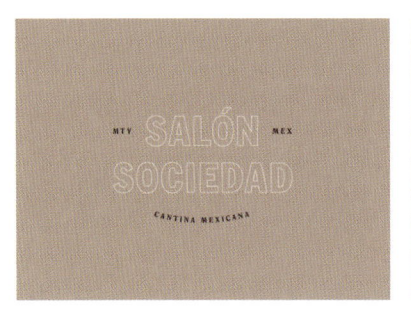
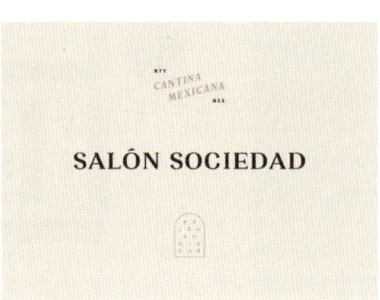

1

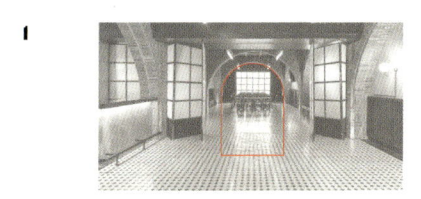

2

3

4

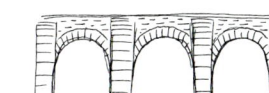

5

6

BONSTINGL

The Bonstingl family is one of the leading construction companies in Austria
It also specializes in the renovation of classic apartment buildings. In keeping
with the artistic craft and the high standards of the company and its clientele
Moodley has placed sophistication, elegance and precision at the center o
its design. A hint of fin de siècle is evident in the Secession-style typography
A royal lion's head in noble hot-foil-embossing gives the design the perfec
finishing touch: an echo of the stucco ornamentation that often decorates th
ceilings and walls of upmarket old buildings.

BONSTINGL

MEISTER DER
ALTBAUSANIERUNG.

1

2

3

4

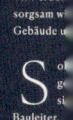

ACHTENDER

Achtender is a fine-dining restaurant located in Metzingen, a small city in Germany. Inspired by the traditional pursuit of hunting, the designer started with the drawing of an elk figure, which he tried to fit within a number of frames of different shapes. The final logo was eventually placed within a red hexagon, which is quite eye-catching. Employing illustration and hand drawn fonts in its branding design, including the one for Achtender, is a distinctive feature of Hochburg. For them, illustration and hand drawn fonts are more creative and artistic and are harder to replicate.

1
2
3
4

Post-80s is a monthly workshop where young designers who were born between 1980 and 1999 gather together to share their experiences and stories about design. The open frame resembling a window indicates that the salon is a platform for open communication. Inside the frame, the designer has created a hollow sans-serif type for the workshop name, which represents the vivacity and energy of young designers, and the Arabic numeral "80" is cleverly embedded in the Chinese characters. The "n" at the upper left of the logo stands for the nth power, implying the infinite potential of the new generation.

1

2

3

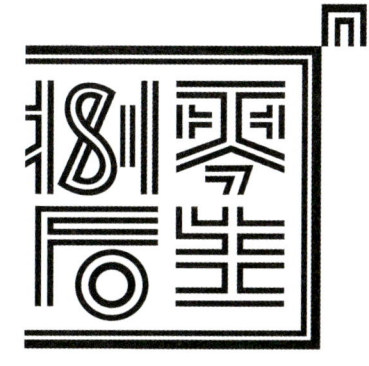

八零后生设计沙龙

DESIGN SALON

TIME/
2013
−6−
−28−

ADD/
贵州上行品牌设计顾问
DESIGN SALON

DESIGNSHOW

AFTER THE DESIGN REVOLUTION

80主义,可畏后生。
它是新锐设计师交流的平台,
汇集设计艺术、文化思潮、创意良品。
它是一种精神,一种力量,一种态度。
它是年轻的战场,亦是成长的讲堂。
它是1980以后,新鲜的设计氧气。

如果你----------------
有勇气、够热血、对艺术情有独钟
如果你----------------
有思想、够独立、对设计苛求完美
那么、快来"秀"出你的"80后生"

80, THE YOUNGER GENERATION WILL SURPASS THE
OLDER.IT IS A CUTTING-EDGE DESIGNER EXCHANGE
PLATFORM,COLLECTION OF DESIGN ART, CULTURE,
CREATIVE QUALITY.IT IS A KIND OF SPIRIT, A KIND OF
STRENGTH, A KIND OF ATTITUDE.IT IS THE YOUNG
BATTLEFIELD, ALSO IS THE GROWTH OF THE
FORUM.IT IS THE 1980 AFTER THE DESIGN OF
OXYGEN, FRESH.
IF YOU HAVE THE COURAGE, ENOUGH BLOOD, HAVE
A SPECIAL LIKING TO ART.
IF YOUTHERE IS THOUGHT, IS INDEPENDENT, TO
DESIGN THE PERFECTTHEN, COME TO "SHOW" YOU
"AFTER 80 STUDENTS"

Designer: Hisham Zeineddine

ARTLAND

Artland is a Saudi-based company operating in a number of fields including design, general contracting and furniture. Based on the golden ratio, the lettermark design, with the use of the initials "A" and "L" from the brand name, creates a visual harmony with an elegant modern feeling.

1

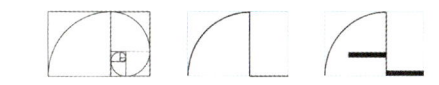

2

3

4

ARTLAND
Interior Design & Contracting

Designer: Anna Nagy (Anakrea)

BATE
ANIMAL SHELTER

With a drawing of a man and a dog holding hands, the designer captures the essence of the relationship between humans and animals. The figure is put into a heart shape, which stands for the sincere friendship and love between the two species.

1

2

3

4

Studio: Suisei / Designer: Kentaro Higuchi

ITO-TENREI

Ito-tenrei is a Japanese funeral company. In Japanese culture, the phoenix is a symbol of the Land of Perfect Bliss. The designer employs a phoenix in the logo to symbolize the peace and solemnity associated with the end of life, and also to honor the deceased. The symmetrical combination of the two flying phoenixes in the logo resembles the hiragana " い ", namely the "I" from the brand name, Ito-tenrei, creating a balanced and harmonious visual result.

1

2

The sound "i"
(the first sound in "Itotenrei").

3

4

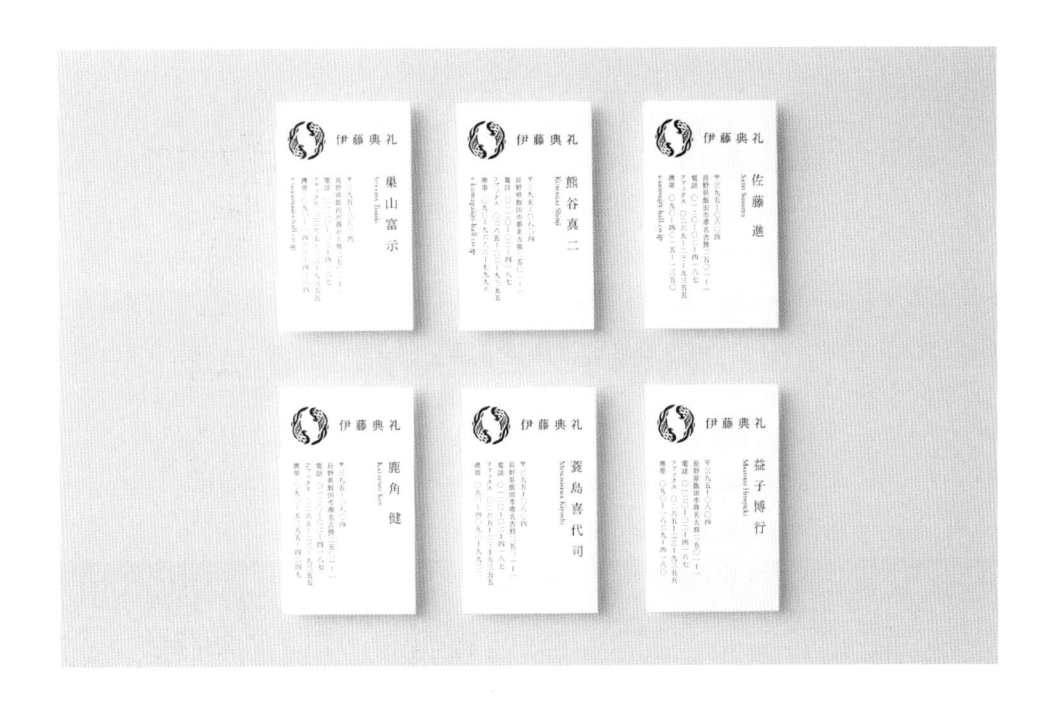

Designer: Jeroen Van Eerden

BROODJE VAN EIGEN DEEG

Four keywords were selected as the basis of the logo design: the letter "B", bread, craft and dynamic. The letter "B", the initial of the brand name, is the foundation of the logo design. With its special design, the "B" appears like a visual representation of bread, with a baguette pattern embedded into its centre. The designer chose a warm brown color, the color of bread, to represent the warmth of the brand.

1

Letter 'B' + Bread + Craft + Dynamic =

2

Beeldmerk + Typografie =

 BROODJE VAN EIGEN DEEG

Designer: Oksal Yesilok

L' OIE

L'OIE is a patisserie in France. The logotype was designed by adding serif to the ITC Avant Garde font, enabling the logo to communicate a traditional and elegant feeling. The bar across the letter "E" is subtly designed into a star symbolizing the spark of inspiration. The logotype is in sweet red, which forms a sharp contrast with the light blue background, enabling a striking visual effect.

1 L'OIE

2 L'OIE

3 L'oie

4 L'OIE

5 L'OIE

6 L'OIE

MOUMA RESTAURANT

Mouma is a modern and pleasant restaurant where you can enjoy live music while dining. The clever use of the fork by the designer not only matches the "M" in the brand name, but also implies the features of the restaurant. In order to create an elegant brand image, the designer chose Slender, a rather concise sans-serif typeface and a simple color palette to go with the unique design of the logo.

1

2

3

Designer: Marlon B. Mayugba

TOKYO CAFE

This is a fresh new look for Tokyo Café, a Japanese-inspired café bar. In the logo design the designer highlighted the symbol of the Tokyo flag instead of the more commonly used icons in Japanese restaurant branding. By incorporating the letter "C" from "cafe" into the icon, a simple but elegant design was brought to life.

1

Tokyo   Cafe   Logo Icon

2

TOKYO JAPANESE
CHARACTER

Symbolizes Sun rising from the East

CARMEN ALVAREZ

Carmen Alvarez is a studio specializing in interior design. The logo design mainly consists of geometric shapes — two squares and a circle — which is inspired by the decoration and design of the studio. The initials of the brand name, the "C" and the "A" are cleverly shaped into two squares. With a black circle as the background, the designer builds up a monochrome logo with a concise yet soft structure, which forms a pleasing contrast with the brand name in a serif font next to it.

1

2

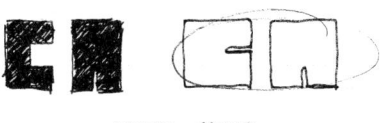

3

4

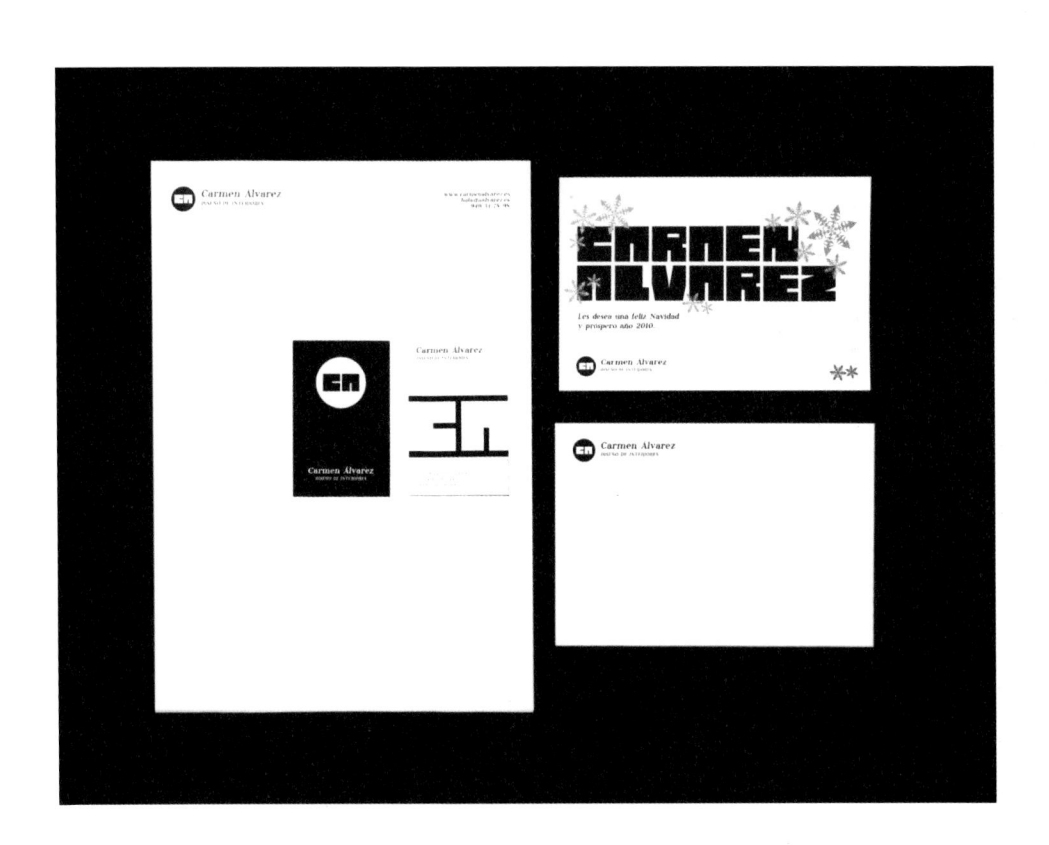

MUSE

Muse, a science museum in Northern Italy, wanted a new identity to reflect the immersive experience it offers. The designer created an angular logotype in a bold and expansive color scheme with a cosmic and geographic influence to represent the museum's position in the Trento valley as well as its universal significance.

1

2

3

4

La forza
dell'esperienza

Museo delle Scienze

MUSe

La forza
dell'esperienza

MuSe

Museo delle Scienze

MANTRA
RAW VEGAN

Mantra is the first raw vegan restaurant in Italy. The logo design is inspired by the concept of the seed. From the seed grows the plant, and the plant in turn produces the seed. Mantra aims at building up a brand image that exudes a sense of simplicity and conciseness. Thus, the designer uses Helvetica Neue, a concise and elegant typeface, for the logo, and each of the letters in the brand name is delicately designed to strip away all unnecessary elements. The bottom of the word "mantra" in the logo is cut off, which makes it look like a plant emerging out of the ground.

1

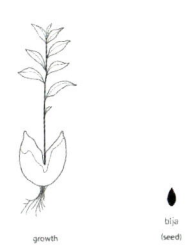

growth   bija
                (seed)

2

mantra
raw vegan

3

mantra

4

mantra
raw vegan

Designer: Xitong Lu

HOUSELIFE FOR LIVING

The brand advocates a simple and back-to-nature lifestyle, so the designer incorporated such elements as a mountain and a river into the logo. The logo design was reduced to the barest detail to honor the brand philosophy — passion for nature and for the local culture. With the use of both thin and thick strokes, and both rounded and right angles, the logo has a vibrant and balanced appearance.

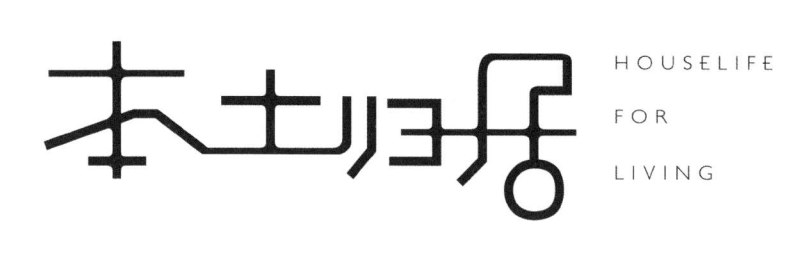

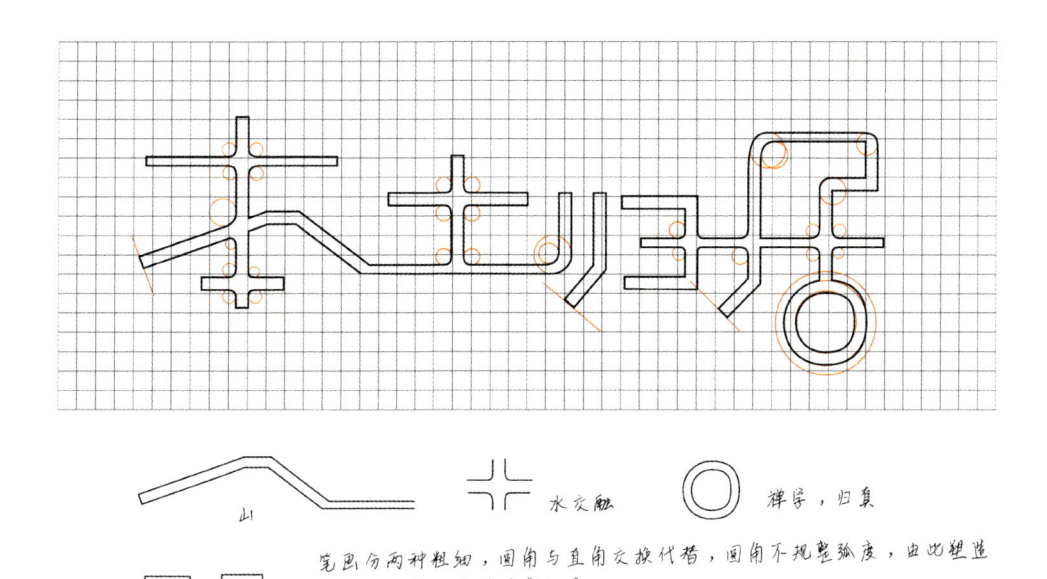

水交融　禅学，归真

笔画分两种粗细，圆角与直角交换代替，圆角不规整弧度，由此塑造自然随性感，再者平衡视觉

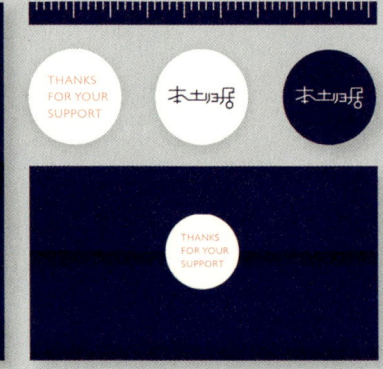

SABADÌ

Sabadì is an Italian chocolate brand. Inspired by Italian advertisements from the 1950s and 1960s, the studio combined the philosophy and the business goal of the brand, and delivered a retro logo design. The sans serif font used in the logo shows the stability of the brand, while the inclined wave shape adds something creative to the logo.

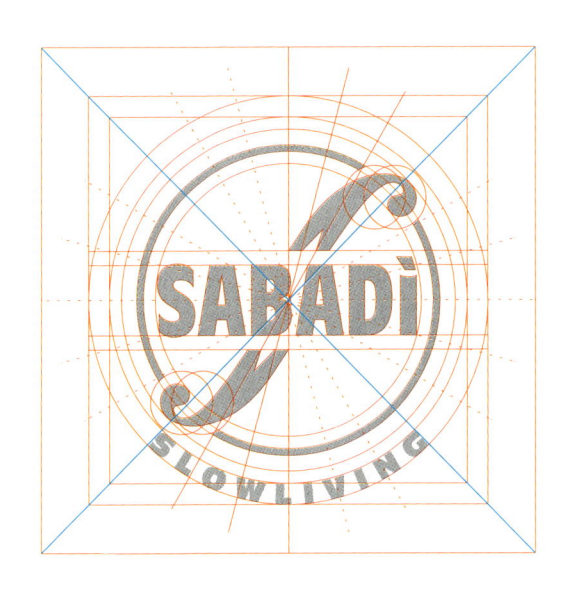

BERNINO
BATATA GOURMET

The logo design for Bernino Batata Gourmet is based on Swiss-style elements. The designer uses the golden ratio as a fundamental rule in the typeface design and employs various kinds of Fibonacci numbers as important basic design components.

1

2

Designer: Daniel Schroermeyer

SPORTSFREUNDE

Because Sportsfreunde wanted to project its brand image as a fun and client-friendly attitude towards fitness and healthy lifestyles, the designer created a lettermark in the shape of a heart, with the letters "S" and "F" in the mark being delicately combined. The logo system is in green, a color that represents health.

1

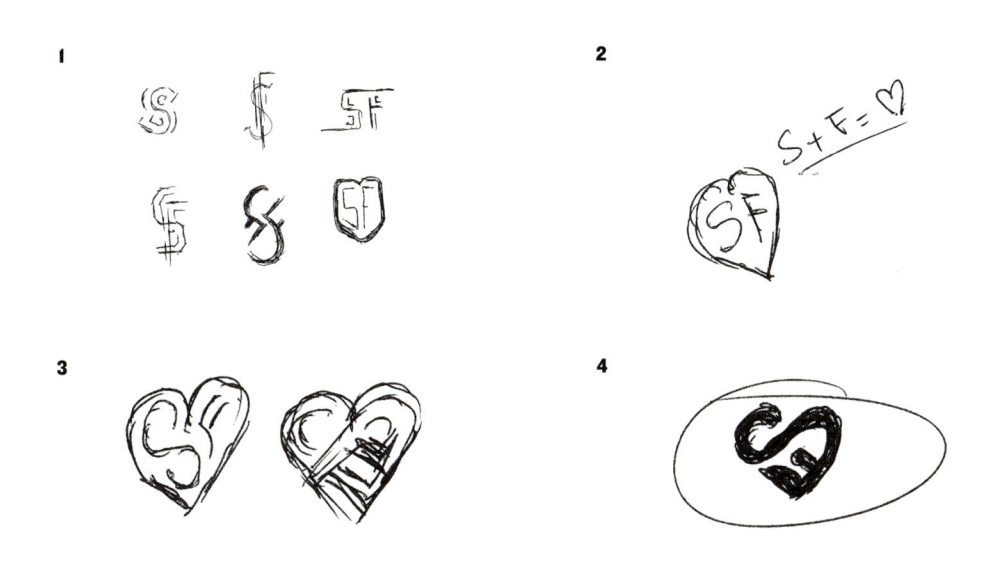

2

3

4

FUJISAN MUSEUM

The designer uses a combination of 8 equilateral triangles to represent the 8 tags of Fujisan Museum — heritage, culture, belief, history, nature, homestay, research and sightseeing. The ingenious piling up of the triangles helps to deliver a classic Fujisan shape, implying a profound meaning in a concise structure.

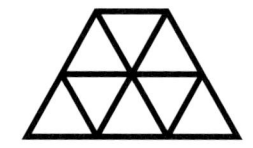

FUJISAN MUSEUM

ふじさんミュージアム

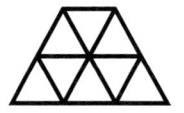 FUJISAN MUSEUM

ふじさんミュージアム

1

 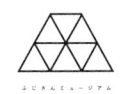   

2

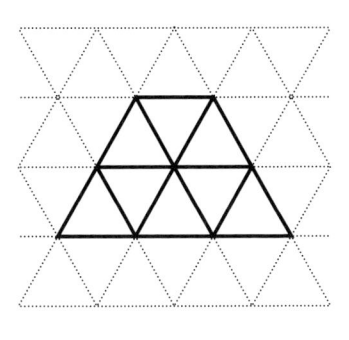

heritage　art　faith　history　nature　folklore　study　tourism

8 ELEMENTS OF FUJISAN (Mt.FUJI)

3

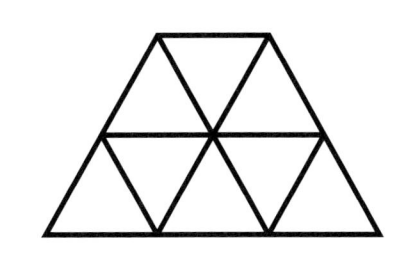

FUJISAN MUSEUM
ふじさんミュージアム

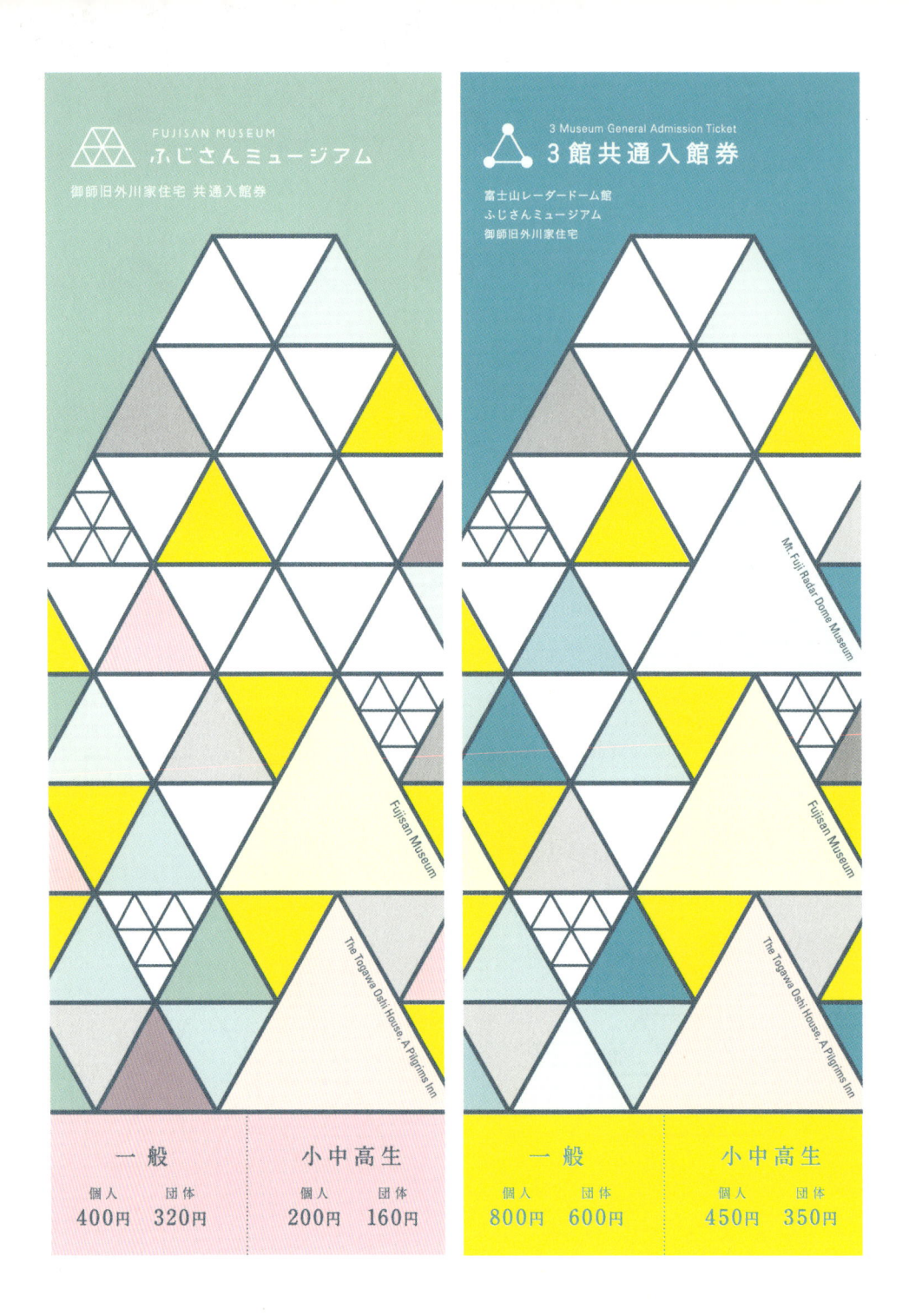

MUNCYT

The inspiration for the logo of MUNCYT (Museo Nacional de Ciencia y Tecnología) comes from the very beginning of all science — questions. The design is based on circles, which generate a dynamic symmetry, hinting at the scientific impulse to never stop exploring questions like "why" and "what is the purpose". Meanwhile, it is an evocative design, echoing such fundamental scientific and technological advancements as the wheel and engines, both of which are related to circles.

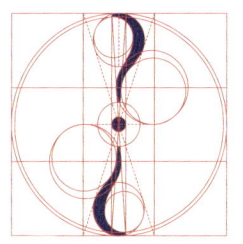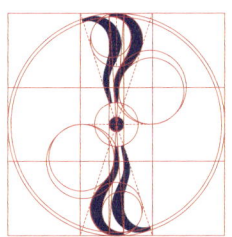

Designer: Álvaro Pérez

CABEÇUDAS

Cabeçudas is a restaurant on a beach in Brazil, providing catering services for parties and weddings. The inspiration for its logo comes from a plate, a fishing net, waves and a sailing boat, all of which highlight the qualities of the restaurant — it is on a beautiful beach, and it offers the best seafood.

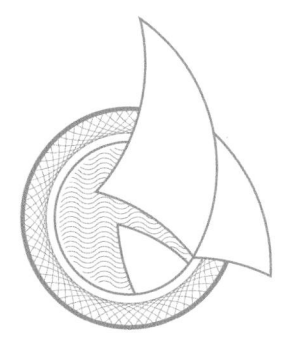

1

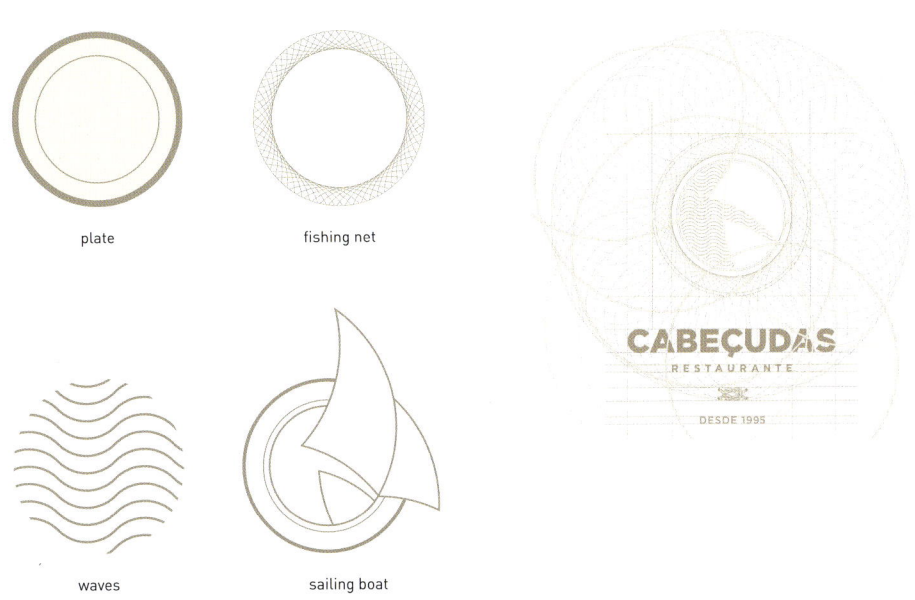

plate

fishing net

waves

sailing boat

2

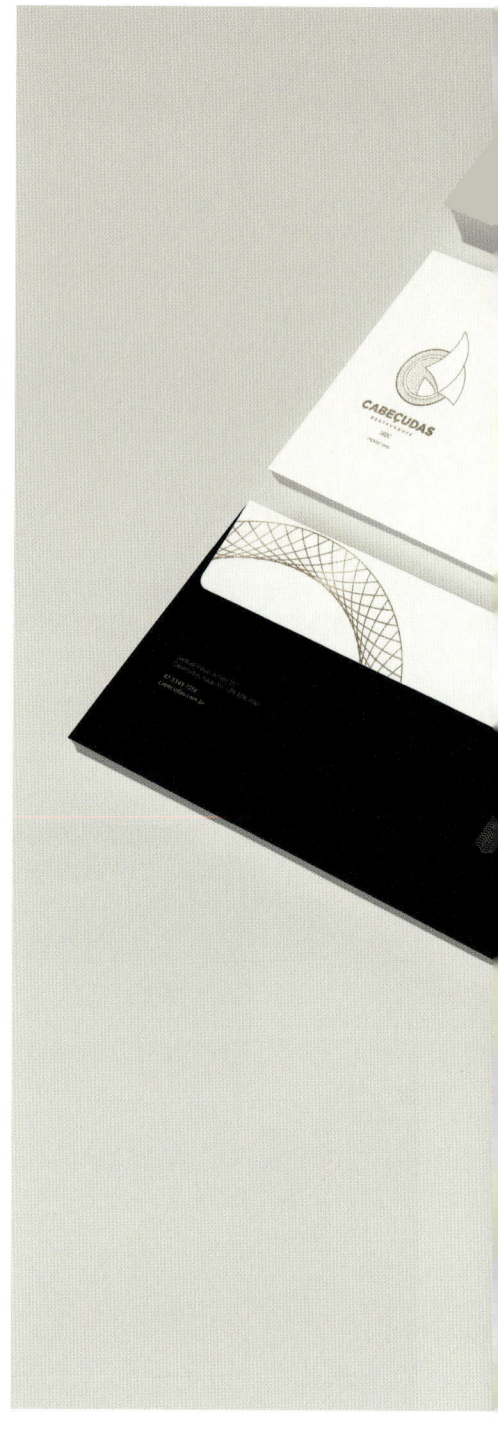

LEAF

Leuser Ecosystem Action Fund (LEAF) is an environmental organization that works to protect critically endangered species and habitats on the Indonesian island of Sumatra. The Leuser Ecosystem is the last remaining location where orangutans, rhinos, elephants and tigers still coexist in the wild. To create impact and a strong connection to what is truly at stake, the designer used the side profiles of the four animals with a clever, yet serious use of silhouette to guarantee recognition and impact.

1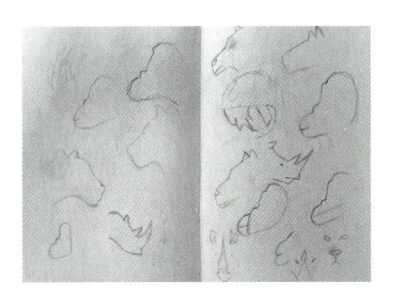

2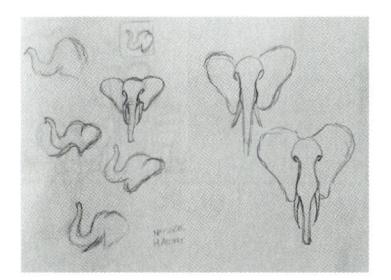

3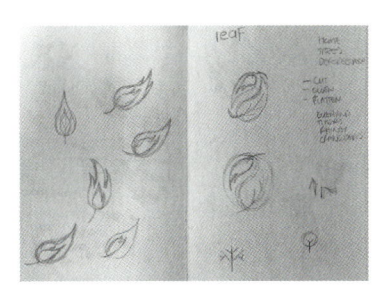

4

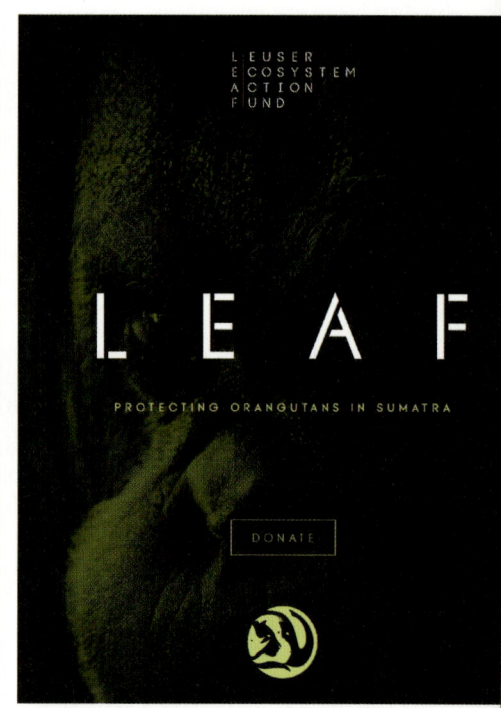

JOSSE ET LUCIEN

The logo consists of a hand-drawn profile of two fictional characters, Josse and Lucien from the brand name. The hand-drawn lines in the logo resemble the sewing thread, which can remind people of the professional services the brand offers.

1

2

Josse et Lucien

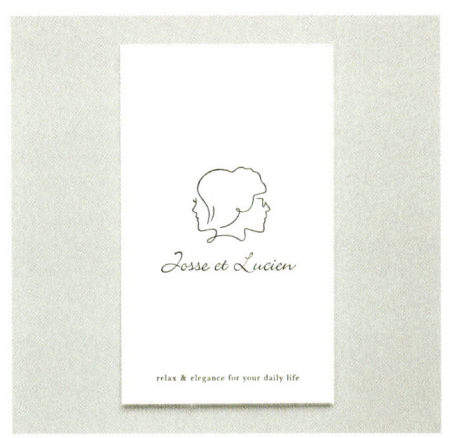

KARMA SUSHI

Karma is a sushi restaurant in Denmark. The logo of the restaurant is inspired by the key ingredient of most sushi — fish, which is shaped into a nicely-proportioned geometric form by overlapping a number of ovals.

1

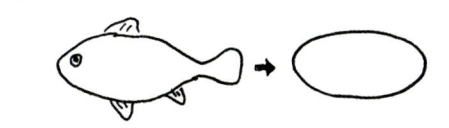

2

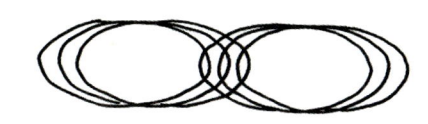

3

4

KARMA SUSHI

Studio: Triangler / Designer: Qiyao Tang, Junyao Huang, Xiangjia Wu, Yi Wang

HANAMIZUKI

Hanamizuki specializes in providing professional office and house cleaning services with its own natural and low-pollutant detergents made from water and oils extracted from flowers and trees. The designers created three geometric shapes to indicate three crucial elements — flower (hana), water (mizu), and tree (ki), the combination of which forms the Kanji " 花 " which skillfully seems to almost respond to the first word in the brand "hana".

1

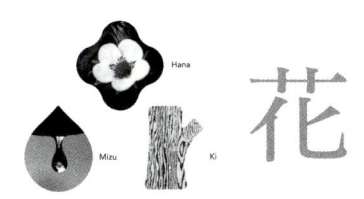

2

3

4

5

6

hana
(flower)

mizu
(water)

ki
(tree)

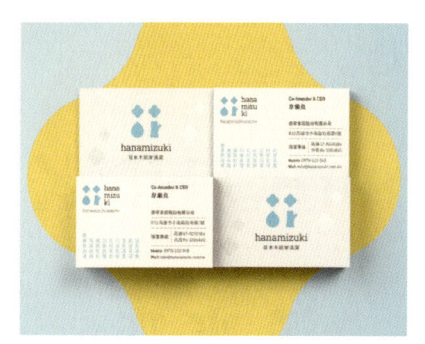

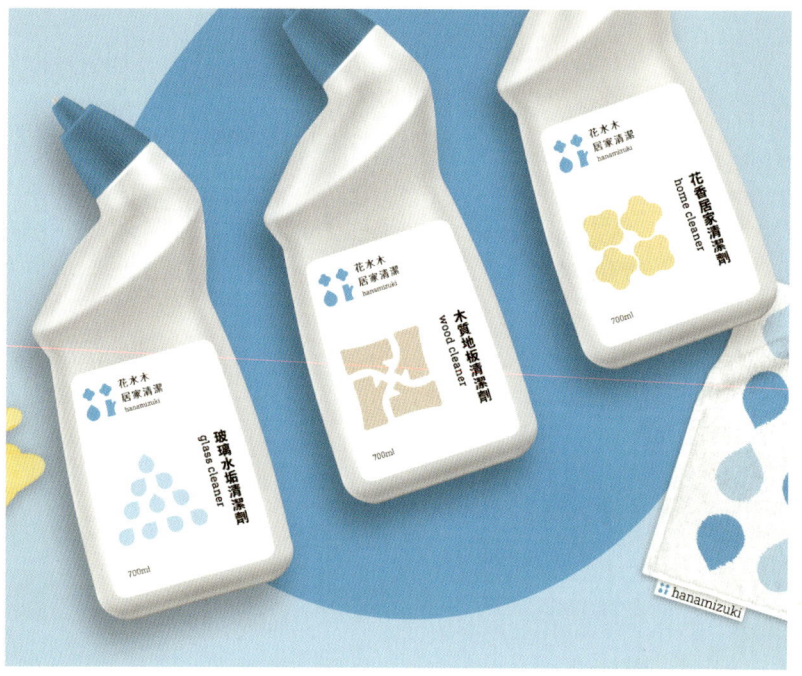

MINIMAL MAMMAL

Minimal Mammal is a luxury brand with high-end product lines for small pets like ferrets, rabbits, hamsters, mice, guinea pigs and hedgehogs. The illustration in the logo features a linear and rounded style. Four animals — a ferret, a rabbit, a hedgehog and a hamster — stand under the arch of a delicately built wonderland, with warmly welcoming smiles. The design reflects the modern and concise style of the brand, and the rose gold used on printed materials is a tribute to this concept of fairy tale.

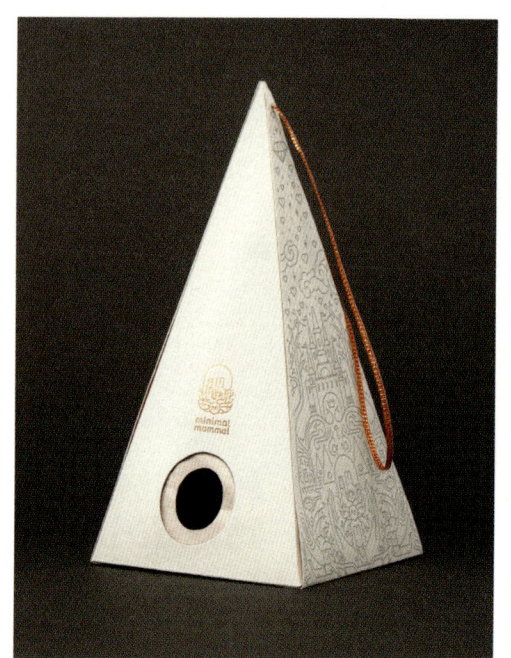

MAREINER HOLZ

Mareiner Holz offers a whole range of techniques for finishing untreated wooden boards in an environmentally friendly way. The woodpecker in the logo represents the agility of the company as well as its pursuit of 100% natural beauty. The designer refined the logo stripping it back to its most essential details with the use of an elegant sans serif font, clearly helping the company to adopt a more focused positioning strategy.

MAREINER HOLZ

BRETTVEREDELUNG

1

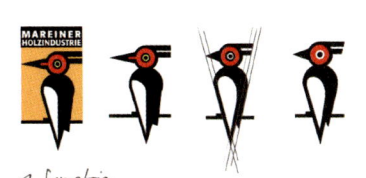

1. Symetrie

2

2. Stabilität

3

3. Reduktion

4

4. Charakter

Designer: Marianella Snowball

COSTA RICA FRUIT COMPANY

Costa Rica Fruit Company is a fruit exporter, mainly dealing in papaya. The logo design is inspired by the seemingly random piling up of papaya shapes. Presented in a light color palette, the logo has a vibrant appearance.

1

2

3

4

Designer: Diana Coe

ANTHOS CONDOMINIUM

Anthos is a condominium management company. The inspiration for the logo comes from the company's philosophy — a condominium is like a living system — as well as the designer's fascination with biomimetics. The designer believes that a condominium with many people living together is like the huge coral that harbors a diverse ecosystem. Thus, she uses coral as the creative basis of the logo.

1

2

3

anthos

166 · 167

Studio: tegusu / Designer: Masaomi Fujita

FORMENTE

FORmente is a Japanese clinic providing comprehensive health care services. The logo is in the shape of a flower, with a delicate combination of four over- lapping circles, each of which represents a petal, as well as one of the four major services the clinic offers. The pistils in the center of the logo resemble the silver needles used in acupuncture. Framed in a circle, the logo is present- ed in a traditional Japanese style, establishing a reliable brand image.

1

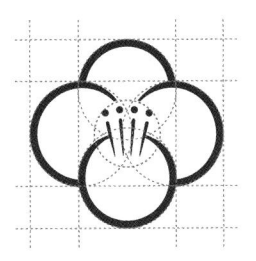

2

3

4

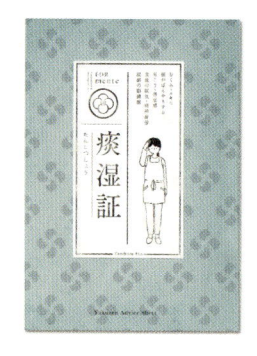

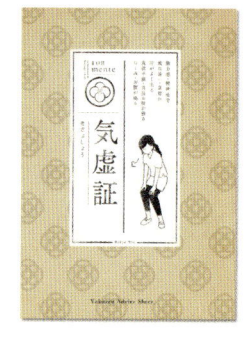
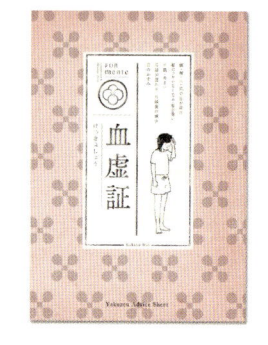

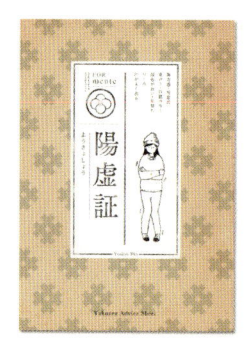
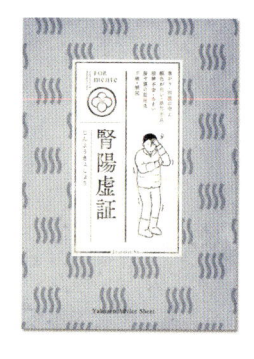

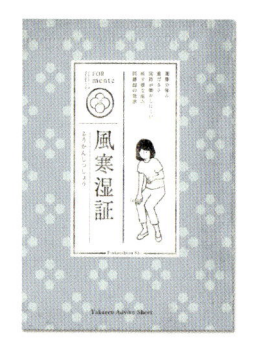

体を根本から
改善するための
4つの施術と
メンテナンス

FOR meute は、新浦安の鍼灸マッサージ院です。鍼治療はもちろんのこと、姿勢調整や、体のメンテナンスに関わることを全面的にサポートし、人それぞれに合った施術法をご提案しています。

鍼・マッサージ acupuncture & massage

原因不明の頭痛や、イライラ/首こり/肩こり、腰痛に悩む各種内臓・筋肉を治療・調整し症状を改善。内側から良いサイクルを生み出す治療を繰り返すことで、内側からあふれる自然な美しさを引き出します。かけていくことで全身のバランスを整えるマッサージ。

美容鍼 acupuncture for beauty

小顔作り、エラ張りやくすみを解消する美容鍼。首のこりや姿勢の矯正、顔のハリをみるみるを治療のバランスを整えながら治療をしていきます。

姿勢調整・歩き方 improve posture

全身のバランスを整え、不調を繰り返さないために、姿勢や、体のクセなどを見直します。おすすめのお茶や食材、レシピが一目でわかる当院オリジナルのカードです。

薬膳アドバイス yakuzen advice

21種類の体質・症状別アドバイスカードを通じて、あなたに必要な食事をアドバイス。おすすめのお茶や食材、レシピが一目でわかる当院オリジナルのカードです。

対象の方
ストレスが強い人
PCやスマホによる首や目の疲れ
疲労がたまっている人
イライラしやすい人
姿勢を整えたい人
全身のバランスを整えたい人
質の良い体作りをしたい人
本来の美しさを引き出したい人

適応症状
肩こり/首こり/倦怠感/頭痛/
腰痛/膝の痛み/むくみ/不眠/
精神不安/お腹の不調 他

施術時間
◎60分／8千円
◎120分／1万2千円
◎150分／1万5千円
※右記よりお選び頂けます

あなただけの
施術プランで

FOR meute
Acupuncture & Massage Clinic

MOON FOX

Moon Fox is a producer of lingerie featuring unique designs and deluxe and comfortable fabrics. The designer started from the brand name, turning the figures of the fox and the moon into line combinations. Foxes are smart and elegant, and evoke sensibility and mystery; the moon has a long-established association with feminine beauty. The combination of the two elements helps to establish a special brand image which gives a lasting impression to its audience.

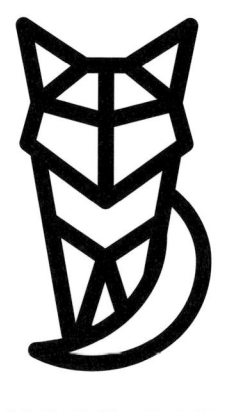

MOON FOX

1

2

3

4

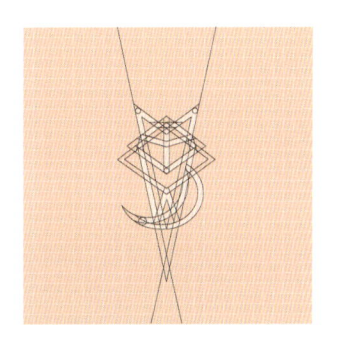

MOON FOX

COME AND TAKE
A WALK ON THE
WILD SIDE

@MOONFOX.CCS

PLUG DESIGN

Plug Design is a Mexico-based industrial design studio. Its logo is a monogram of the letters "P" and "D". They are delicately combined, and shaped into a plug, which represents the electronic gadgets and industrial design that the studio specializes in.

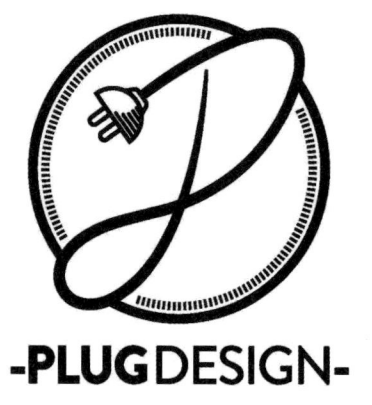

1

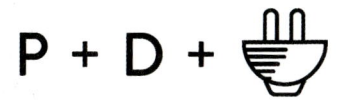

P + D + 🔌

2

3

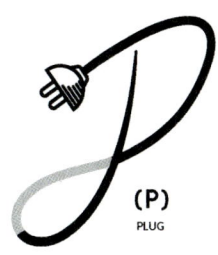

(P)

PLUG

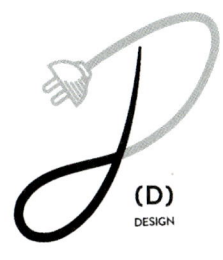

(D)

DESIGN

BROS HAIR

Bros Hair is a hair salon. Its logo is a lettermark consisting of the initials "B" and "H", with a scissor shape hidden in it to show its service field. The design as a whole impresses people with a refreshing feeling and at the same time, the brand philosophy is implied — make customers satisfied and happy.

1

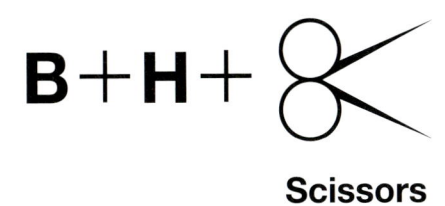

Scissors

2

Designer: Peltan-Brosz Roland

RAWGANIQUE

Rawganique is a brand specializing in producing chemical-free clothing and home textiles. The logo design of the brand is strictly standardized with the use of grids, mirroring its commitment to strict production standards. In the logo, the closed loop shape, a signal of recycling, represents the environmental awareness and humanistic care the brand wishes to project.

1

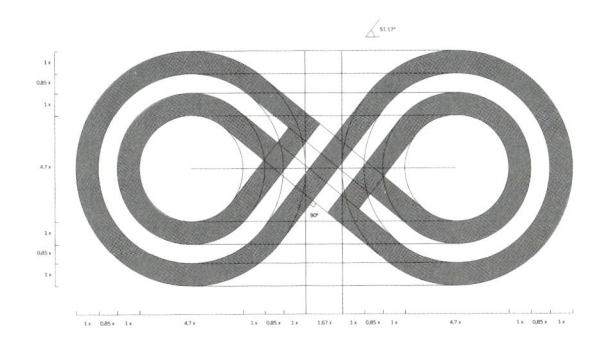

2

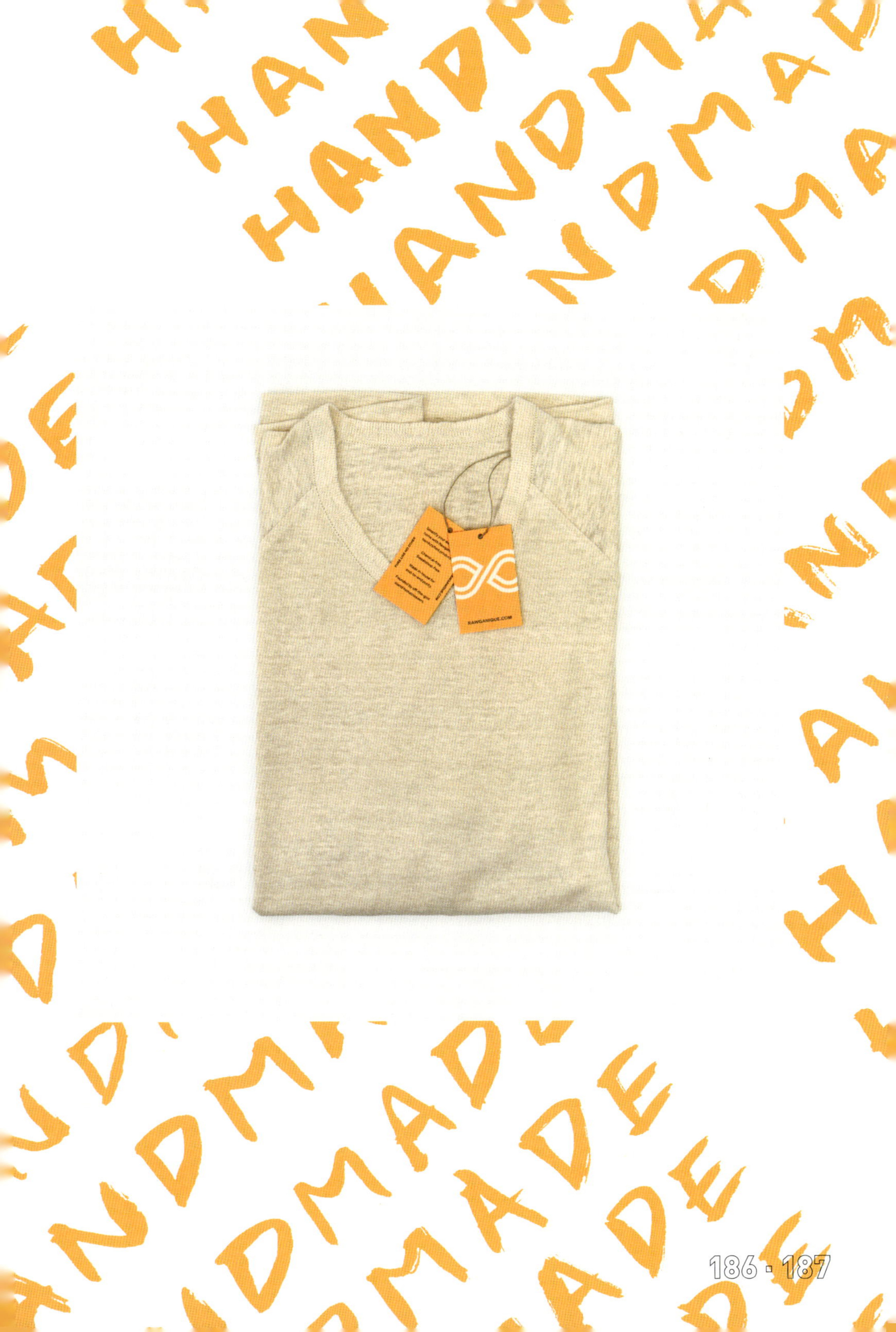
HANDMADE
RAWGANIQUE.COM

MONDELLO PARK

Mondello Park is the only international motorsport racing circuit in Ireland. The logo design was inspired by the starting grid and the arches of a racing circuit. The circle also embodies a core element in motorsport — the wheel. Together, the logo represents the speed of the race and imbues the brand image with a sense of exclusivity.

1

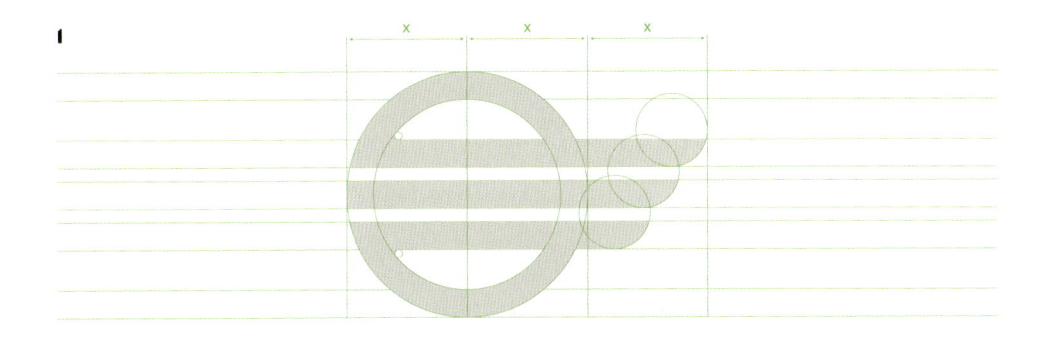

2

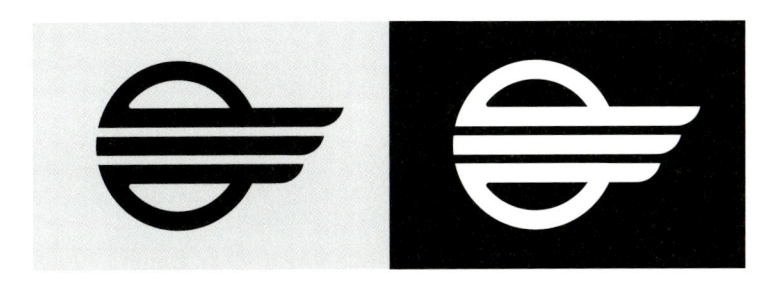

ESTÉTICA D' MARIE

Estética D'Marie is a hair salon exclusively for women, specializing in elaborate braids and ornamentation with natural flowers. The logo design aims at inspiring confidence in the customers with a delicately designed flower as the main body. The color palette uses an autumn tone with a soft and feminine touch.

1

2

3

4

Designer: Gonzalo Cortijo / Illustrator: Juan Dellacha

OWLY

Gonzalo Cortijo developed the brand identity system and the user interface for Owly, a concept app that offers a streaming service with superior audio quality and user experience. From its logo to its modern and intuitive interface, Owly's visual universe stands out for its simplicity — a simplicity that communicates almost naturally with a universe of colors, characters and textures.

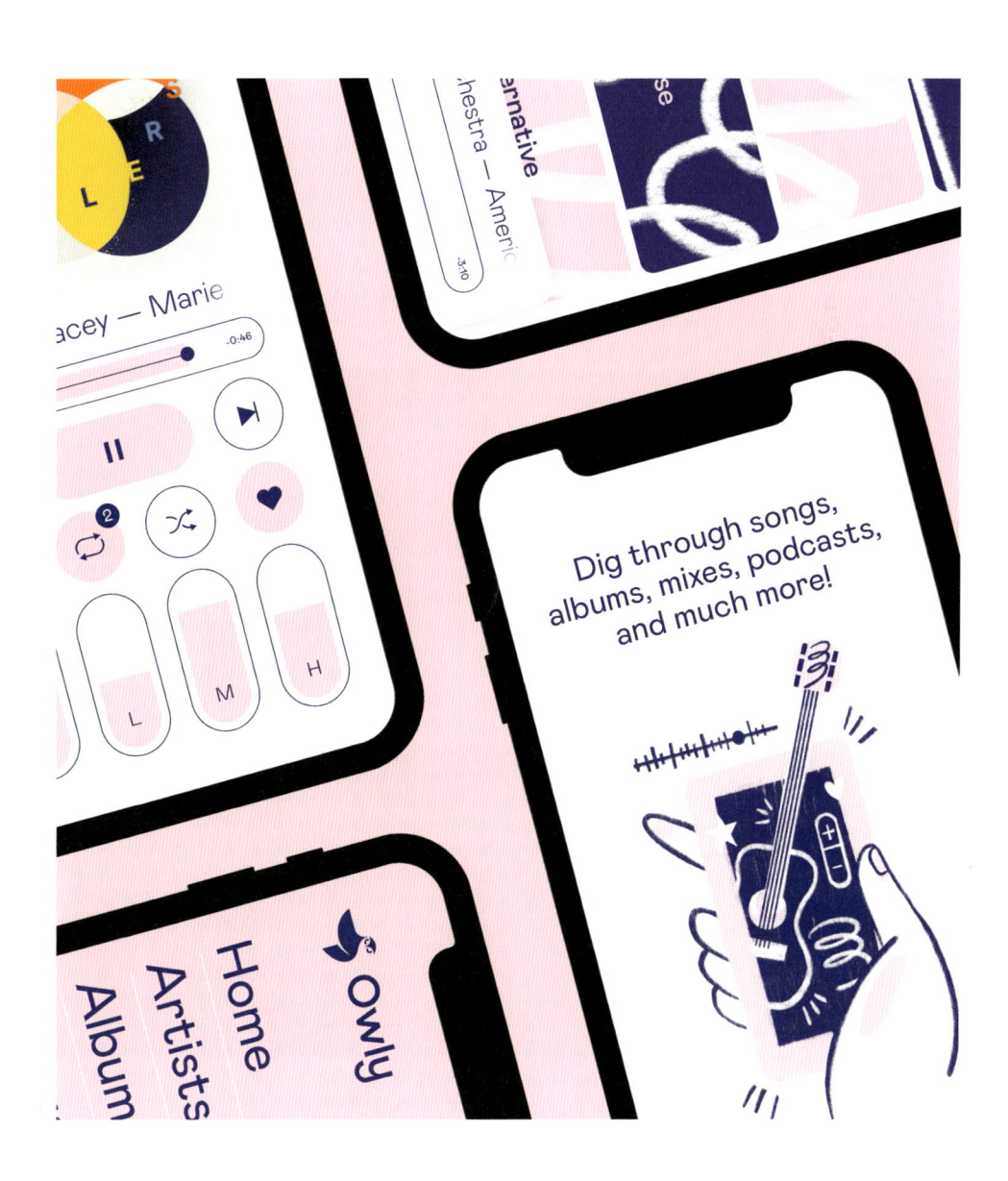

Designer: Yuta Takahashi

CHIYONOKAME

Chiyonokame (meaning Thousand-year Turtle) is a Japanese brewery boasting over 300 years of history. In the redesign project, the designers designed an abstract, modern logo by mixing the "S" from Japanese sake, and the "T" from turtle, to create a simple logotype to go with the concise logo design.

1

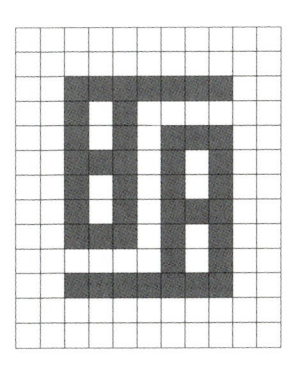

2

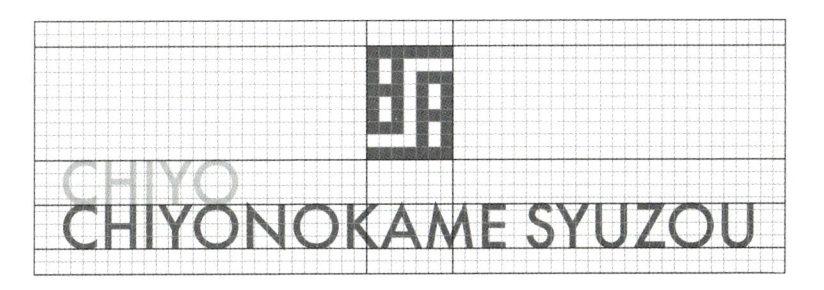

MULTIMEDIA ART MUSEUM

Multimedia Art Museum is a Russian state museum dedicated to the presentation and development of actual art related to new multimedia technologies. The modular logo is rather flexible, as it boasts a number of variations, and it is easy to scale up or down. The design was inspired by Malevich's Black Square, by the screens of smartphones, by televisions, and by App icons, all of which are square, representing the modern world.

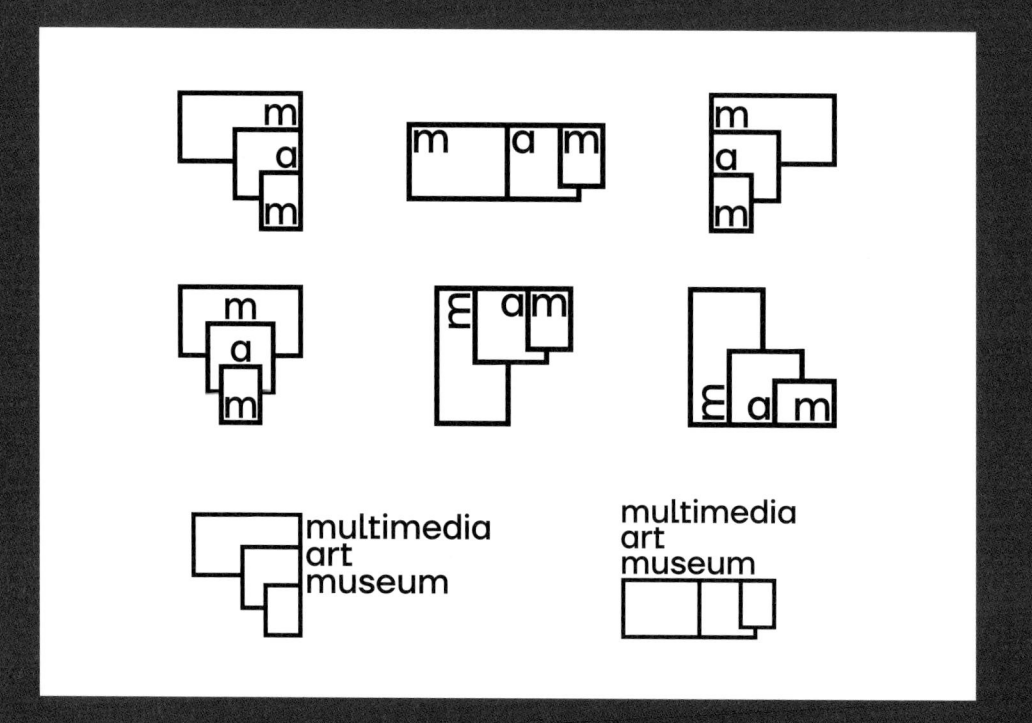

1

2

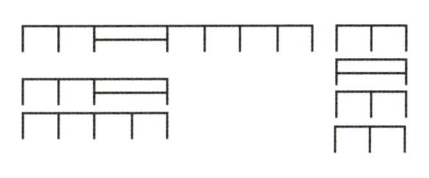

3

4

5

6

7

multimedia
art
museum

8

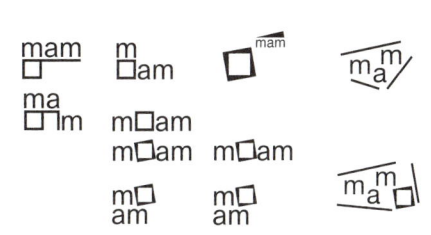

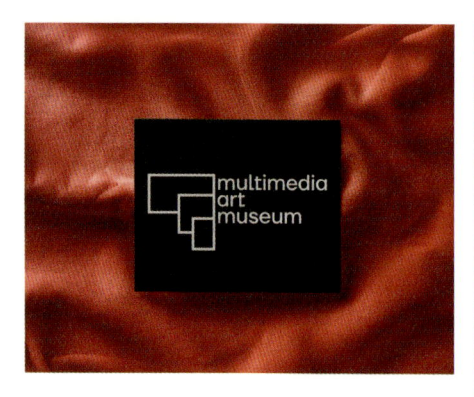

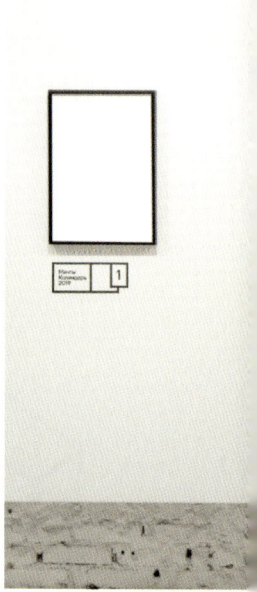

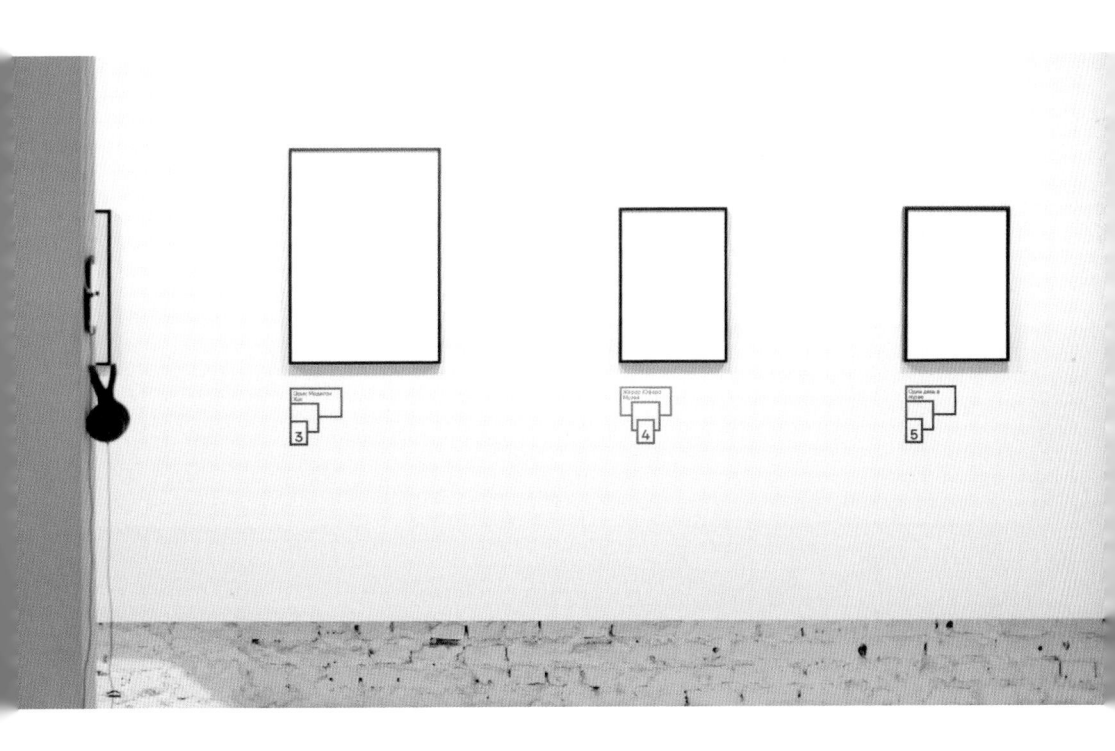

ARK LEAGUE

Ark League is a newly established X-sports global competition. Its logo is simple, modern, and highly recognizable, which is appropriate for X-sports events. Thus, the designer took inspiration from things like the human body, energy and passion, as well as movement and competition, and related the idea to the tournament's theme "Noah's Ark".

1

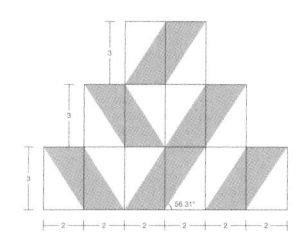

2

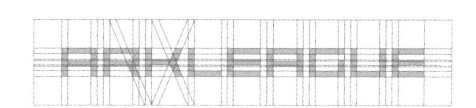

3

LA ROCCA

La Rocca specializes in the latest high-end fashion eyewear, eye care and comprehensive eye tests. The design is inspired by vintage optometrist test glasses, with the two circles in the logo symbolizing people's eyes. The lines on one of the circles represent double vision and blurred vision. The two circles come together to create a central focal point with a clear direct vision — better eyesight as a result of the services La Rocca provide.

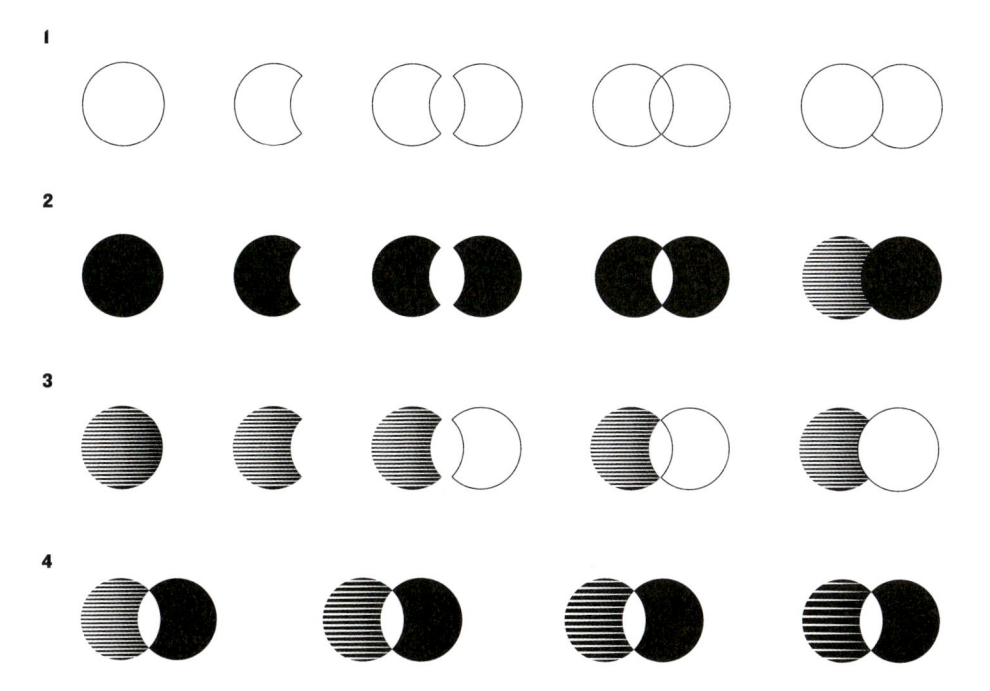

LA ROCCA
EYECARE

LA ROCCA EYECARE
34 WELLS ST FRANKSTON 3199
03 9783 9920   VINCE@LAROCCAEYECARE.COM
LAROCCAEYECARE.COM

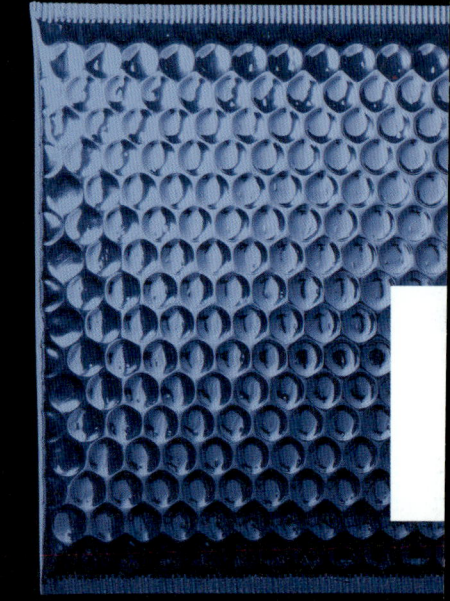

VINCE
OPT

DATE

LA ROC
34 WELLS
03 9783 9920   VIN
LAROCC

LA ROCCA
EYECARE

LA ROCCA
...CCA
...RE

...STON 3199
...RE.COM

AUTUMN / WINTER
NOW IN STORE

LA ROCCA
EYECARE

LA ROCCA EYECARE
34 WELLS ST FRANKSTON 3199
03 9783 9900   VINCE@LAROCCAEYECARE.COM
LAROCCAEYECARE.COM

ARPE

Arpe specializes in microfiber products and has a long-standing tradition and a significant role in design and innovation. The new logo takes inspiration from three of the keywords of their business — weaving, confection, and stamping — to consolidate the company's new presence in the market.

1

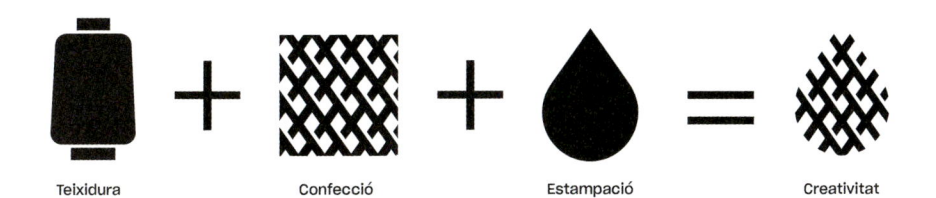

| Teixidura | Confecció | Estampació | Creativitat |

2

3

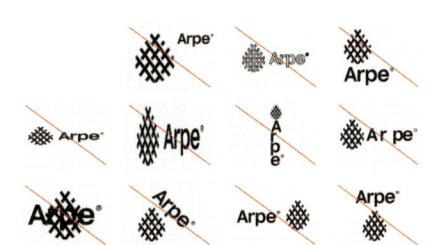

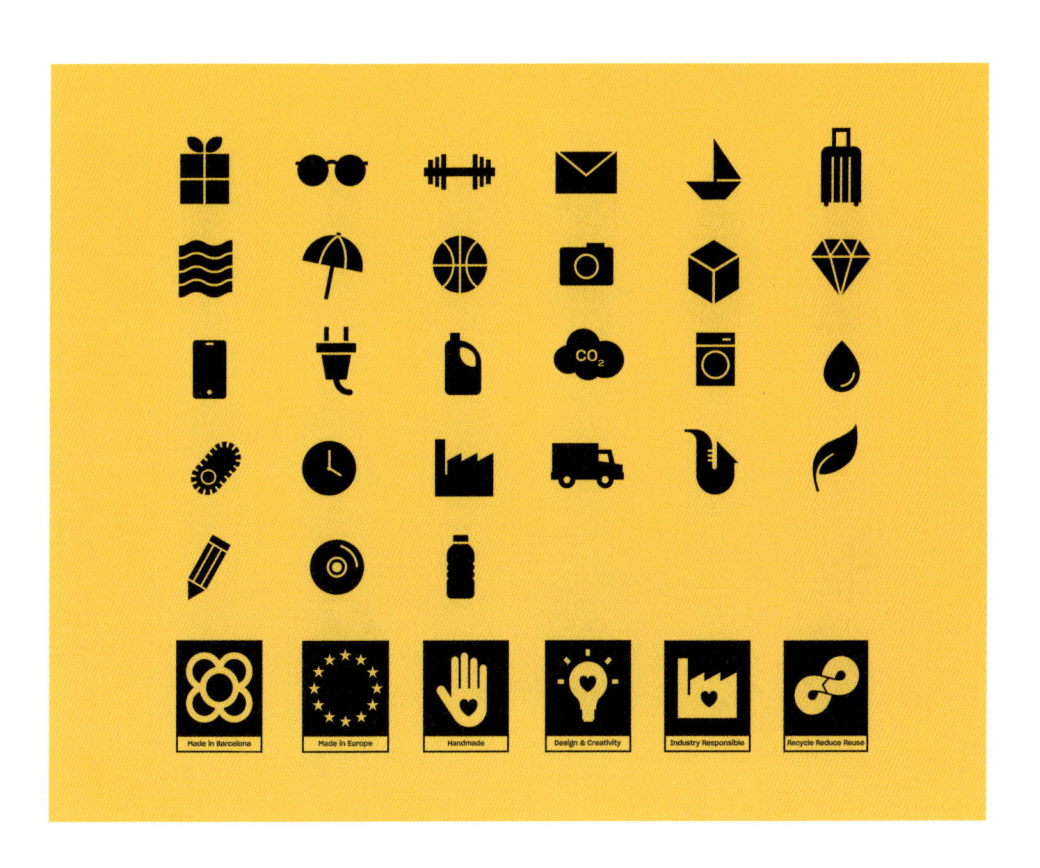

ESTÚDIO FRENTE

This logo is an ambigram, highlighting the features and techniques of the brand's craftsmanship. Though it keeps the characteristics of an artistic font, the sketch is based on strict and precise geometric grids. As a result, the logo, taking its inspiration from Fibonacci numbers, appears both vibrant and structured. The studio decided to go with a varnished and embossed iteration in printing without adding any color when the logo was applied to the brand's stationery. In this way, the logo can be closely related to the materials it is printed on.

1

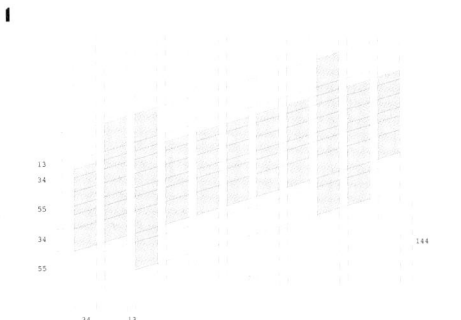

2

3

4

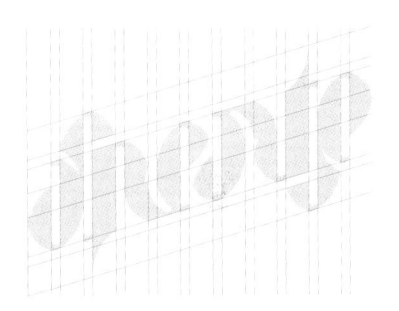

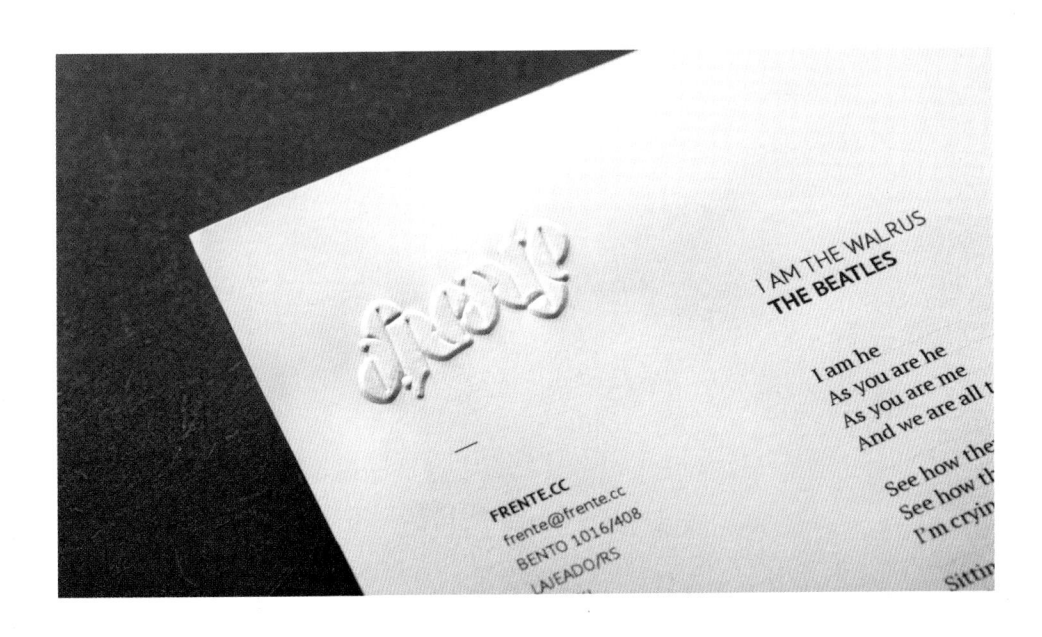

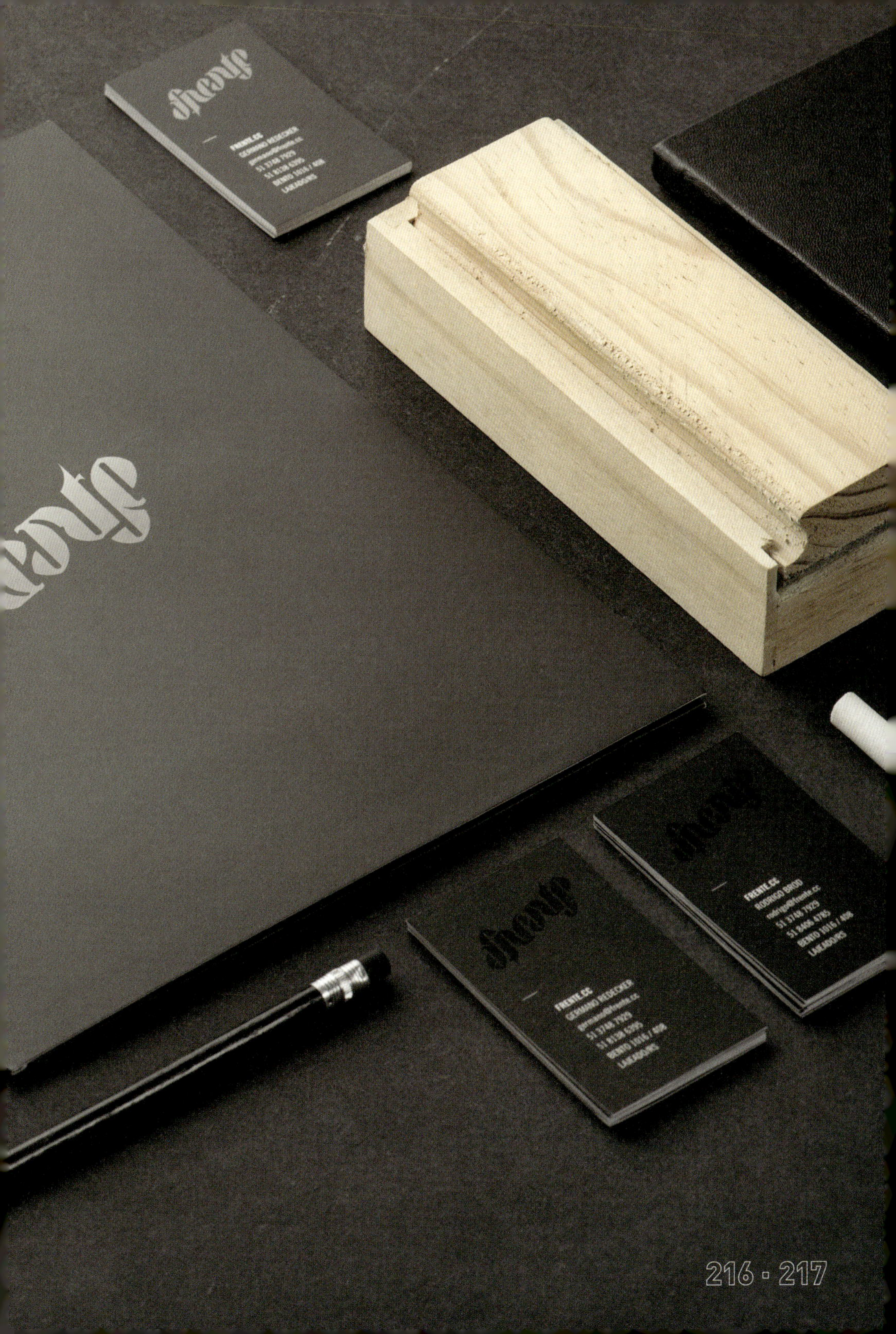
FRENTE.CC
GERMANO REDECKER
FRENTE.CC
RODRIGO BROD

BRIGHTON BAKERY

The designer selected a color palette of apricot and brown, which is similar to the color of the bread. Combined with the initials of the brand name, Brighton Bakery, the logo looks like freshly baked bread. The warm color tone makes people feel warm, creating a comfortable and friendly atmosphere that the bakery wishes to project.

1

ブライトン
ベーカリー
Brighton Bakery

2

ブライトン
ベーカリー
Brighton Bakery

3

ブライトン
ベーカリー
Brighton Bakery

Designer: Gonzalo Cortijo

DECLIT

Declit is an Argentinian company dedicated to the design, manufacturing and marketing of lamps and lights. Inspired by Bauhaus's use of geometric forms, the designer developed a simple, elegant yet visually strong brand mark. Based solely on circles, the brand mark is highly recognizable and flexible enough to work in different environments, applications and sizes, with a shape that closely relates to its business.

1

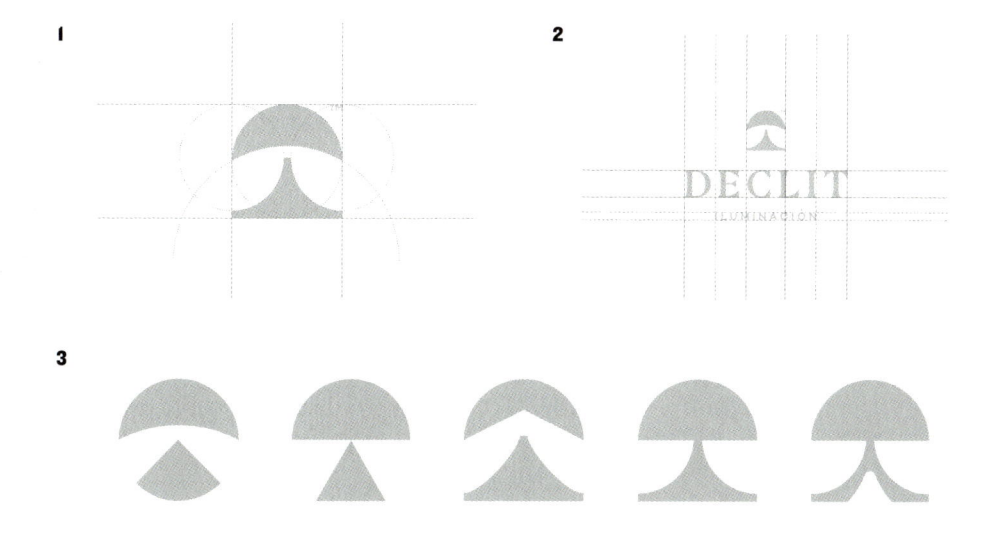

2

3

Teatro & Punto is a Chilean website dedicated to literature and theatre. The logo design consists of simple geometric shapes which resemble the tip of an ink pen and the stage, features of its two domains, literature and theatre. The brighter and the darker parts together function as the connection between the two disciplines, and represent black ink and white paper, as well as the light and shadow of a theatre stage.

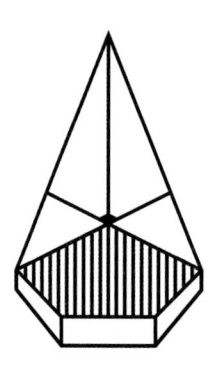

TEATRO & PUNTO
literatura ~ dramaturgia

1

2

3

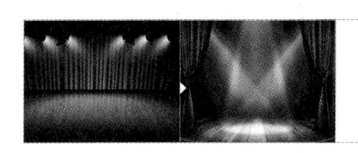 

4

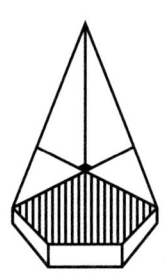

224 · 225

Designer: MILTZ

GOKOU & SUMI-GOKOU BRANDING

The GOKOU Series, blending five varieties of high quality sweet potato, has a fruity flavor despite the fact that it is a liquor made from potatoes. The name refers to "five red glows" and symbolizes the five sweet potatoes used in brewing the strong "GOKOU" and the easy-to-drink "Sumi-GOKOU". The design and typography of the two series maintain a consistency of style, but there are small differences in the detail, with solid lettering for GOKOU and softer outlines for Sumi-GOKOU to represent the different flavors of the two series. The designer also developed stamp-inspired marks for each variety of sweet potato to emphasize the five varieties used.

1

2

安納芋
Anno potato

3

紅はるか
Beni-haruka

4

シルクスイート
Silk sweet

5

エイムラサキ
Ei purple potato

6

宮崎紅
Miyazaki-beni

 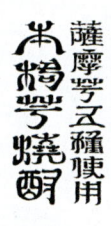 

薩摩芋五種使用
本格芋焼酎

Sumi GOKOU

［一升／十四度］

GOKOU

［一升／二十五度］

GOKOU

Sumi
GOKOU

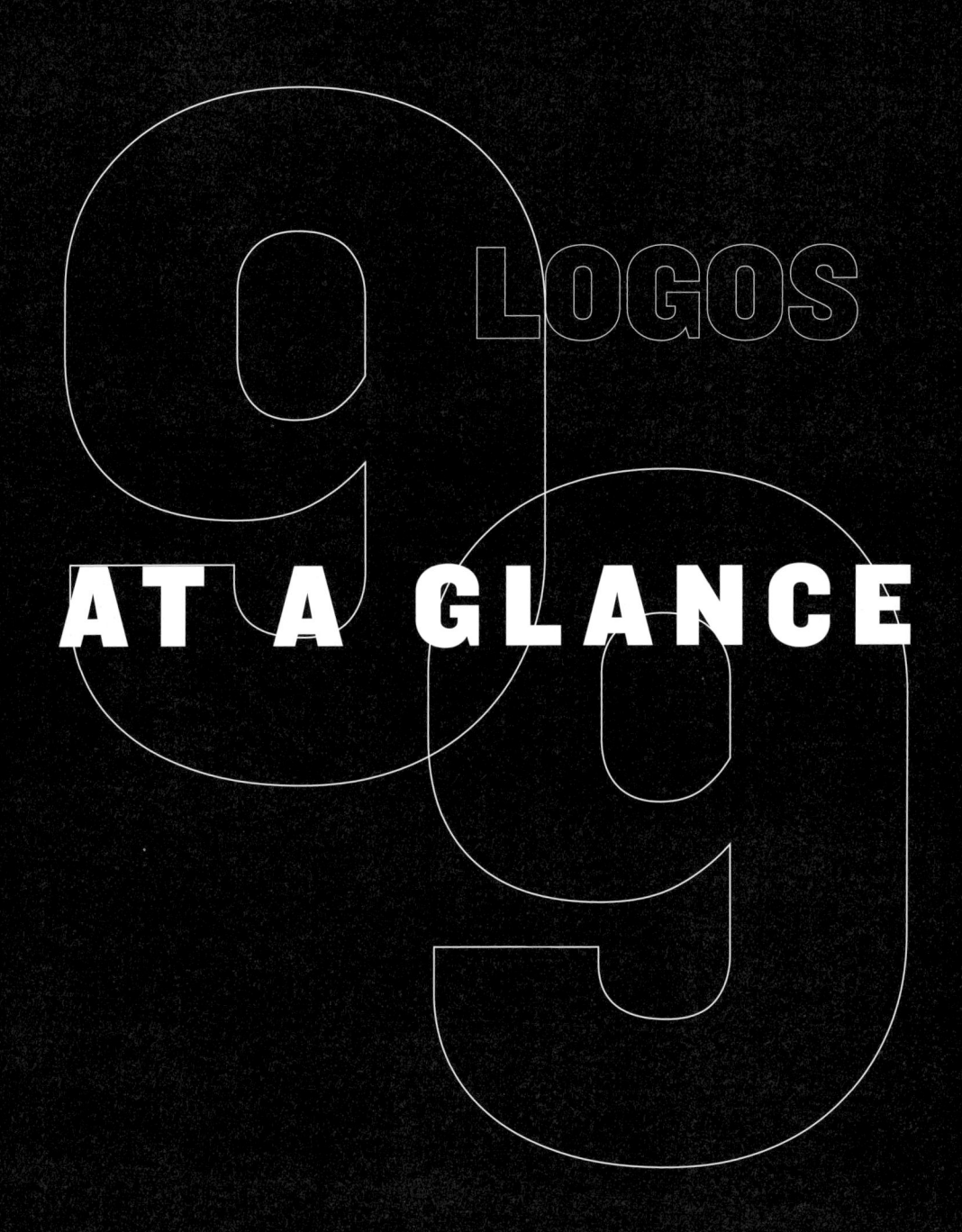

9 LOGOS AT A GLANCE

01 de:work

02 quattrolinee

03 Toormix

04 Unfold

05 Studio AIO

06 Drew Watts

07 Jacek Janiczak

08 Matthias Deckx

09 Hochburg

10 Infinito

11 Studio Daad

12 Polygraphe

13 Estúdio Gilnei Silva

14 Giada Tamborrino

15 Menos es Más

16 Mireldy

17 Reut Ashkenazy

18 Ahmad Ghassan

01

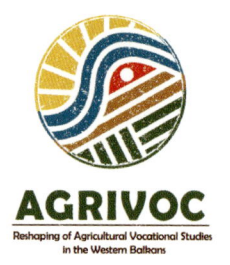

02

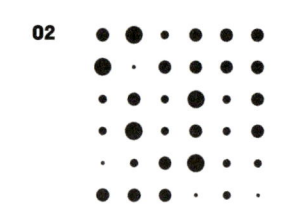

03

04

05

06

07

08

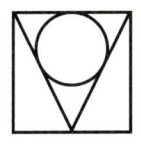

MOK
Specialty Coffee
Roastery & Bar

09

INVEST IN HEADS

10

BEM BOS

11

12

KOMBI

13

VINERIA

14

MOKA

15

16

DRAP. AGENCY

17

Ufficio

18

DREAM PALM RESIDENCE
Unlock Your Dream House

19 Forma & Co

20 Sense

21 United Design Practice

22 Lara Khoueiry

23 Valerio Scarcia
Graphic Design

24 The 6th

25 Anagraphic

26 tegusu

27 Igor Bubel

28 the brandbean

29 the brandbean

30 CRE8 DESIGN

19

20

21

22

23

24

25

26

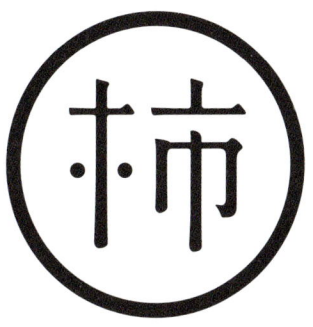

Kakino Kinoshita

27

28

29

30

3 1 DPIGS & Gilberto Ribeiro

32 Anagrama

33 Half Mountain Design

34 SPREAD

35 BRAND BROTHERS

36 reformer

37 Estudio Menta

38 Denkstudio

39 Superfried

40 Corey James

4 1 Matt Erickson

42 tegusu

31

32

33

34

35

36

37

Café Restaurante Bar
Df
SVAGO

38

ФЕРМА БЕНУА
ресторан

39

cuta rug

40

THE COTTESLOE
BEACH HOTEL

41

BOOMER PIZZA
BAXTER, MN

42

もりした♪
音楽教室
Morishita Music School

43 Gonzalo Cortijo

44 Diana Egri

45 Anna Nagy (Anakrea)

46 Creative Technology
Art Studio

47 Stylo Design

48 Yueming Zheng

49 de:work

50 Antoine Gadiou

51 Studio AIO

52 tegusu

43

44

45

46

47

48

53 Carla Sartori

54 Giuseppina Grieco

55 MAMBO art & design

56 Ginger Monkey

57 thonik

58 AM Design Studio

59 Punk Your Brands

60 Arithmetic

61 manuel de simone

62 Leonor de Almeida

63 Y-DESIGN

64 Nuri Cha

53

54

55

56

57

58

MONTES CO
Arte & Diseño

59

Kennedy's
coffee

60

AMOLA
TABLE TOP NECESSITIES FOR LAND AND SEA

61

BAS∖
M∖NT

62

HÒBÁLÁ

63

64

BLOSSOM

65 Small

66 Oliver Hambsch

67 Oliver Hambsch

68 Oliver Hambsch

69 Oliver Hambsch

70 12 points

71 Oliver Hambsch

72 Oliver Hambsch

73 Oliver Hambsch

74 Oliver Hambsch

75 The Comeback Studio

76 tzke

65

66

67

68

69

70

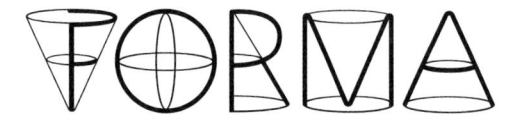

71

72

73

74

75

76

77 Anoniwa

78 AM Design Studio

79 MAROG Creative Agency

80 Gaba Jordan

81 Navarra.is

82 Julie Song Ink

83 Cam Altamura

84 Chad Roberts Design

85 Para Todo Hay Fans

77

Cilsoie
PRIVATE BIJOUX

Cil Soie Délicatement

78

79

80

81

TREE OF TEA

82

83

84

85

86 Luka Balic

87 Mission Design

88 Nayane Nathalie

89 Codoro Studio

90 Esteban Oliva

91 Happy Design

92 This is Pacifica

93 Side by Side

94 Ines Cox

95 One Design

96 Leo Vinković, Goran Šoša

97 One Design

98 Helix Advance

99 de+st studio

86

87

88

89

90

91

RISORGIMENTO
DI MILANO

92

ArchiDesign
Studio

93

94

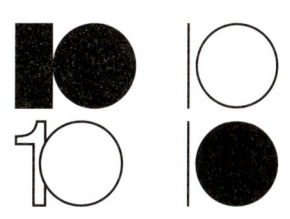

96

KLINIKA
BIKE SERVICE & SHOP

95

TALKIN' THREADS
LIMITED EDITION

97

BLOWHAMMER

98

Cut
point

99

NORDIC FOOD

INDEX

Álvaro Pérez
www.alvaroperez.es
P130, 134

Anna Nagy (Anakrea)
www.behance.net/anakrea
P086

BigO
www.bigo.ie
P188

BULLET Inc.
www.bullet-inc.jp/
P126

Changhong Shi
www.sch2013zf.zcool.com.cn/
P078

Communal Studio
www.communal.mx
P066

Daniel Schroermeyer
www.dlrm.co
P122

Diana Coe
www.dianacoedesign.com
P164

El Taller M
www.eltallerm.com/
P192

Germano Redecker
www.behance.net/germanohr
P214

Gonzalo Cortijo
www.gonzalocortijo.com
P194, 222

H

Happycentro
www.happycentro.it
P114

Hermes Mazali
www.hmazali.com
P054

Hisham Zeineddine
www.hishamzeineddine.com via Internet
P082

Hochburg
www.hochburg.design/
P074

HUESO
www.Hueso.co
P062

J

Javier Muñoz Poblete
www.javierdg.com
P224

Jeroen van Eerden
www.jeroenvaneerden.nl
P090

K

Kasper Gram
www.kaspergram.com
P144

Kirill Dubrovsky
www.be.net/dbrvsk
P200

KOM Design Labo
www.design-kom.com
P180, 218

L

Lucia Nolasco
www.untextoquesirvadepretexto1.
tumblr.com
P058

M

Made&Co.
www.behance.net/scottchang
P050

Mai Creative
www.maicreative.com.au
P206

Marianella Snowball
www.nelasnow.com
P160

Marlon B. Mayugba
www.behance.net/marlonmayugba
P096

MILTZ
https://www.behance.net/miltz
P228

Moodley
www.moodley.at/en
P070, 156

Nugno
www.bynugno.com
P188

Oksal Yesilok
www.oksalyesilok.com
P092

Oscar Bastidas (Mor8)
www.mor8graphic.com
P172

Pablo Chavida
www.pablochavida.com
P094, 100

Para Todo Hay Fans
www.paratodohayfans.com
P176

Pata Studio
www.patastudio.uk
P152

Peltan-Brosz Roland
www.Peltan-brosz.com
P184

Pentagram Design
www.pentagram.com
P102

Rodrigo Brod
www.r.brod.com.br
P214

Roger Lara
www.lyon-branding.com
P058

S

Samyr Paz
www.rpfaz.com.br
P214

Suisei
www.suisei-suisei.com
P088

Supercake (Srl)
www.supercake.it
P106

Superfried
www.superfried.com
P138

T

tegusu
www.tegusu.com
P142, 168

Toormix
www.toormix.com
P210

Triangler Studio
www.triangler.com.tw
P148

Triocom
www.triocom.com.br/
P118

Xitong Lu
www.lxt-design.diandian.com/
P110

Yuta Takahashi
www.yutatakahashi.jp/
P198, 204

© 2021 SendPoints Publishing Co., Ltd.
First printing of the first edition, January 2021

EDITED & PUBLISHED BY SendPoints Publishing Co., Ltd.
PUBLISHER: Lin Gengli
PUBLISHING DIRECTOR: Shijian Lin, Nicole Lo
CHIEF EDITOR: Shijian Lin, Nicole Lo
DESIGN ADVISOR: Ting Chen, Dongyan Wu
EXECUTIVE EDITOR: Weiji Li, Baomin Huang
EXECUTIVE ART EDITOR: Ting Chen, Chow Pakwah
PROOFREADER: Baomin Huang, Chujun Huang, Michael Farrelly

REGISTERED ADDRESS: Room 15A Block 9 Tsui Chuk Garden, Wong Tai Sin, Kowloon, Hong Kong, China
TEL: +852-35832323 / **FAX:** +852-35832448
OFFICE ADDRESS: 7F, No.9-1 Anning Street, Jinshazhou Road, Baiyun District, Guangzhou, China
TEL: +86-20-89095121 / **FAX:** +86-20-89095206
BEIJING OFFICE: Room 513, 5th Floor, Building 1, Longde Zijinjia, No.186 Litang Road, Changping District, Beijing, China
TEL: +86-10-84139071 / **FAX:** +86-10-84139071
SHANGHAI OFFICE: Room 302, Floor 3, Ningbo Road no.349, Huangpu District, Shanghai, China
TEL: +86-21-63523469 / **FAX:** +86-21-63523469

SALES TEAM
TEL: +86-20-81007895
EMAIL: sales@sendpoints.cn
WEBSITE: www.sendpoints.cn / www.spbooks.cn

ISBN 978-988-79284-2-3